GETTING PAST YOUR BREAKUP

GETTING PAST YOUR BREAKUP

How to Turn a Devastating Loss into the Best Thing That Ever Happened to You

Susan J. Elliott, JD, MEd

A Member of the Perseus Books Group

Designed by BackStory Design
Set in 11.25 point Adobe Garamond

Cataloging-in-Publication data for this book is available from the Library of Congress.

First Da Capo Press edition 2009
ISBN: 978–0–7382–1328–6

Published by Da Capo Press
A Member of the Perseus Books Group
www.dacapopress.com

Note: The information in this book is true and complete to the best of our knowledge. This book is intended only as an informative guide for those wishing to know more about health issues. In no way is this book intended to replace, countermand, or conflict with the advice given to you by your own physician. The ultimate decision concerning care should be made between you and your doctor. We strongly recommend you follow his or her advice. Information in this book is general and is offered with no guarantees on the part of the authors or Da Capo Press. The authors and publisher disclaim all liability in connection with the use of this book. The names and identifying details of people associated with events described in this book have been changed. Any similarity to actual persons is coincidental.

Da Capo Press books are available at special discounts for bulk purchases in the U.S. by corporations, institutions, and other organizations. For more information, please contact the Special Markets Department at the Perseus Books Group, 2300 Chestnut Street, Suite 200, Philadelphia, PA, 19103, or call (800) 810–4145, ext. 5000, or e-mail special.markets@perseusbooks.com.

LSC-C

30 29 28 27 26 25 24 23

For my children,

Christopher, Michael, Nicholas, and Gina

Success is building a foundation
with bricks thrown by others.

DAVID BRINKLEY

ACKNOWLEDGMENTS

No author can write a book alone, and I've had plenty of support. So there are many people I'd like to thank:

My husband, Michael DiCarlo, for loving me, being there for me, and believing in me like no one else ever has. I love you truly.

My beautiful grandsons, C.J. and Derek, for giving me a reason to smile every single day.

My brothers, Ricky and Billy. I love you.

My best friend, Carlotta Cassidy, for her unwavering understanding and support.

My dear friend Barbara McCarthy for always being there.

My supportive friends Marian Erickson, Candice Cook, Melissa Wandersee, Jenny Rynell, and Martin Pascual.

My daughters-in-law, Kristen and Heather, and my sisters-in-law, Kathy and Marion.

My mentors, teachers, and inspirations along the way: Cheryl Cabral, Beverly Hall, Rodney Hayes, Ken Hammond, Katie Sunderland, Jacquie Pells, John James of the Grief Recovery Institute, and Lou Tice of the Pacific Institute.

My agent, Diane Freed, and the great group of people at FinePrint Literary Management.

My editor, Katie McHugh at Da Capo, for believing in this book.

Joan and Anthony Nittoli, Theresa Andis-DiCarlo, Mark Carley, Julie Carlo, Tony Nittoli, Joe Jasniewski, Kathy Fox, Vonne Cranmer, Gia Goldman, Lexi Feinberg, Beatrice B., Nick Chiodini, Eric Elkins, Brenda Murphy, Laura Jelin, Eileen MacDonald, Kara Harter, Jenny Mahoney, Gena Wright, Patrick Lidji, L. Felipe Guimaraes, Paul Alexander, Megan MacLeod, Lucy Hunt, Libby Huegel, Heather Baker, Nicole Cusick, and Genevieve Sebesta.

All my blog readers, seminar students, private coaching clients, and conference attendees, as well as all of those who encouraged me to "put it in a book."

I've spent twenty years researching and reading, but there were a few books that touched my heart and soul, changed my life and had a profound effect on my work. I'd like to thank the authors of those books: Melody Beattie, Robin Norwood, Susan Forward, Clarissa Pinkola Estés, Therese Rando, and Stephen and Ondrea Levine.

After I finished writing this book, Michael, the love of my life, was diagnosed with terminal brain cancer. Although facing his loss is devastating, I would never have known the love of such a special person if I had not changed my life. The years I have spent with him have been the best I've ever known. I am caring for him as he would do for me if the situation was reversed. I will be forever grateful that he came to share my life. And that would not have been possible without the work described herein.

CONTENTS

PREFACE: MY STORY

> It is by going down into the abyss that we recover the treasures of life. Where you stumble, there lies your treasure.
>
> JOSEPH CAMPBELL

The following stories of my relationships and of my childhood are extreme, but I tell them for you to believe that if I can do it, you *can do it. I have a life today that not only is successful but is absolutely joyous. I am healthy, happy, and strong. I've done the work that I ask you to do in the following pages. I know that it's hard, but believe me, it's so worth it.*

When I ended my marriage, I was convinced it was the right thing to do for about twenty-four hours. I had been unhappy for a long time, the fights had become unbearable, and I was convinced he was cheating on me. Although I had lived with my husband's criticism for years, things grew much worse when my company went bankrupt and I suddenly lost my job.

My boss gave me a good reference, and I tried to think positively in the first few days after the layoff. I edited my résumé, bought an interviewing suit, and researched potential employers. But each night my husband would come home expecting a clean house and a cooked dinner, since I was "home all day doing nothing." Arguing with him was the last thing I needed, so I put the job search aside and spent the next few days cooking and cleaning. He then took issue with the "simple" meals I made and the fact that his clothes were not washed. When I spent the next day doing laundry and making an elaborate midweek meal, he complained that I wasn't actively looking for work and barked at me for "playing house."

This type of no-win situation was nothing new in our relationship, but without my job to distract me, it began to grate on my nerves. I was stressed over money and my professional future and didn't need someone haranguing me over meals and laundry.

One day I thought I had hit upon the perfect balance. I went on a job interview in the morning and when I came home I waxed the floors. While the floors dried, I picked up the kids from school and brought his favorite take-out food home. I had looked for work, cleaned the house, spent time with the kids, and had a surprise dinner waiting for him. I was sure I had hit the home run of domestic bliss.

He came home that night and pointed out that there were streaks on the floor and accused me of purposely messing up the floors so that he would not "let me" do it again. I was stunned and tried to explain that was not my intention. It reminded me of my mother's criticism when I was a kid. She said that I purposely screwed things up to shirk my responsibilities. Hearing the same thing, I insisted that was not what happened. He called me a few choice names, and I retaliated with names of my own. As had become the norm, the argument grew violent and we each threatened to end things once and for all.

The next day I told him it was over and he had to leave. He scoffed at the idea and blamed me for what had transpired on the previous night. Whenever our arguments escalated into violence, it was my "fault." Most of the time I believed him, but this time I didn't care whose fault it was. I just wanted it to end.

I packed a box of his things and left it on the kitchen table with a note telling him to take it and leave. Instead of arguing with me, he grabbed the box and stormed out. I felt an immediate sense of relief—I was so glad to be alone.

But in the morning I could barely lift my head off the pillow. At first I thought I was sick, but soon realized there was nothing physically wrong. Forcing myself out of bed to get the kids to school, I felt more than a little sad. As the day wore on, I tried to stay busy to brush off an encroaching feeling of doom. With each passing hour, I found myself increasingly glancing at the phone. By the early afternoon, I was checking it every few minutes to be sure it had a dial tone.

As the boys played, I arranged some chicken in a pan. Instead of my usual jeans and T-shirt, I put on a skirt and a blouse, applied a thick coat of mascara, and brushed my hair up to one side. I secretly hoped that he would come home and see a cooked meal, a clean house, a lovely wife, and quiet children and want to move back in. *What?* I had tried to get out of this relationship for a long time. *Why was I thinking these bizarre thoughts?*

For the next few days, he didn't call or come over, and I stopped eating and sleeping. I felt dazed, anxious, depressed, and obsessed with thoughts of him. Instead of concentrating on our recent battles, I relived the good times of our relationship. Missing him desperately and realizing that I had made a horrible mistake,

I tried to get in touch with him so we could talk. He didn't answer any of my messages.

One afternoon he walked through the door unexpectedly, looking for a few things and asking about the boys. The conversation started off slowly, but then I blurted out, "Please come home." I cried and begged him to come back. Unmoved, he sneered at me and turned to leave. I ran after him, trying to wrap my arms around him, imploring him not to go. He shoved me hard and walked out the door. I sat on the stairs, humiliated and weeping uncontrollably. My life was over if I could not find a way to make him come back.

In the morning I was determined to clean the house, find a new job, and cook an exquisite dinner. Instead of asking him to return, I would just show him that I meant everything I said. I would coax him by being a good wife, a good mother, and a good earner. Bounding out of bed, this was the day to start my life over and get my husband back.

I fed the boys, got them off to school, and then it was time to tackle the house. Everything looked clean, but I was going to make it sparkle and shine.

After I washed the boys' breakfast dishes, I pulled a new yellow sponge from its cellophane, dipped it in cleaner, and proceeded to scrub. As I moved the sponge across the kitchen counter, it occurred to me that it was already clean. Growing up, I would clean the house from top to bottom to please my mother, but inevitably she would find the one thing that was out of place or the one corner that was messy. It had been the same way since I married my husband. So now I asked myself, "How clean is clean enough?" And the answer coming back was, "I have no idea."

As I scrubbed, tears began streaming down my cheeks. "Is this clean enough? Is this good enough?" My mutterings turned into rants and the rants turned into screams, "When is it clean enough? When is it good enough? When am I good enough?" Then, suddenly, I collapsed on the floor.

I was physically unable to move under the weight of the realization that I had no idea who I was or what I wanted. I didn't know what "clean enough" was and I didn't even know if I liked everything "clean enough." I had known families who were perfectly content with messy houses and no one was punished or castigated for it. Maybe I wanted to be one of those people. Maybe I wanted to be someone who really didn't care either way. Maybe I cared but wanted to have a housekeeper clean for me. But here I was, scrubbing a spotless countertop not because it really needed to be clean, but because I was trying to win approval from people who had never really approved of me.

What did I like? What did I think? When did I stop having an opinion?

Suddenly I was propelled backward to my first memory at age three or four: waking up from a nightmare where the "bad people" were taking me away. As a foster child, I would dream that evil creatures in dark garments were grabbing me out of my bed.

Growing up, I heard many rumblings suggesting that my foster family would not be able to adopt me. I also visited with my birth mother occasionally and met two of my brothers and played with the oldest, Edward. I couldn't figure out whether I would be better off with my birth family or my foster family. I didn't feel as if I belonged in either family and waited for cues from others as to what I should do and where I should go.

One day, when I was seven, I walked into the visiting room at the Catholic Charities office. My mother sat on a chair, my youngest brother next to her, and Edward played in the corner. I went over and sat next to him, and he silently offered me one of his toys. We didn't talk but smiled at each other now and again. His eyes were a little sad, and he seemed like a kindred spirit. I had no idea that would be the last time I would see him. Shortly thereafter, my mother relinquished me for adoption.

After years of traveling to the Catholic Charities office to see my mother, I spent the last subway ride away from there imagining my life out of the limbo of foster care. When the papers were signed, I was enthusiastically looking forward to being a "normal" American kid. In fact, we went to dinner that night to celebrate the beginning of my new life. Born at the age of eight! I was thrilled.

But the bubble burst shortly thereafter. All was not well at home. My adoptive father was a drinker, and when my mother smelled alcohol on him she would begin to rage. When he would not react to her anger, she would threaten to drown herself in the East River or lock the bathroom door and say she was going to swallow all the pills in the medicine cabinet. I would listen in horror as my adoptive mother—the only one who had been there for me—swore that she was going to kill herself. Even when there were not dramatic threats of suicide, the arguments would go on for hours until he walked out of the house. She would turn her wrath on us, and we would scramble for cover or try to make things look "nice" in the house so she would stop being so angry.

We did also have some good times when my parents were in sync. Forgetting about the horrible fights, we would go to movies, or out to eat, or spend a night at home playing cards. But soon enough my father would start drinking, my mother's shouts would pierce the calm, and there would be pandemonium once again. By the time I was ten, I had learned that a nice night was really just a pause in the fighting. By the time I was twelve, I had learned that nothing was as it appeared to be. By the time I was fourteen, I really didn't know much of anything.

The influence of my parents and my early experiences was soon evident in my teenage attractions to boys who were either abusive like my mother or absent like my father. By age eighteen, I was in a relationship that was not only abusive, but potentially lethal: When he drank, there was a good chance he might kill me. Incidents in the relationship included several black eyes, being choked until I blacked out, and being locked in a closet for two days. After he let me out of the closet, I tried to take off down the street, and he attempted to run me down with my own car. My life, bad as it had always been, had officially disintegrated into a horror movie.

Finally, I got out and moved safely away from him. Shortly thereafter, I reunited with a friend of mine, the man who would be my first husband. Once again I was looking for the elusive "normal" life and whatever the thing was that would turn me into a normal person. I thought that if only someone loved me enough, I could be normal and happy.

As I stared up at the ceiling, I began to realize that I had held on to my dead marriage to avoid this parade of awful memories. The chaotic patterns of my relationship—the cyclical breaking up and making up—kept me from dealing with all the abandonment, abuse, and grief. Into the void created by our separation and the loss of my job came this pile of horrible thoughts, feelings, memories, and unfinished business. I couldn't deal with this enormous pile, this daunting task. I needed help. And fast. I called a therapist and babbled my desperation into the phone, and although she was booked for weeks, she told me to come in the next day.

Having arrived almost an hour early, I sat in the parking lot, chilled to the bone and wondering if I was making the right move. Finally, I went in at the appointed hour. The therapist was small, thin, and young with a turned-up nose, perky smile, and strawberry blonde hair pulled up into a swinging ponytail. I wondered what in the world this little person could do for me. She motioned to the chair across from her and asked me to tell her why I had come. My voice quivered and grew small as I recounted how wrong I had been to end my marriage. In between wracking sobs, I talked for a half hour. Then she stopped me and asked what was wrong with my face.

My face?

My life was falling apart and she was worried about my face? At first I tried to ignore her and go on to something else but she kept commenting on my appearance. My clothes were messy; my hair was stringy and kept falling in my broken-out face. When I wouldn't answer her because I didn't know how, she said, matter-of-factly, that what she saw before her was a person with no self-worth and no self-esteem. Not *low* self-esteem, but *no* self-esteem.

I told her I didn't care about my self-esteem; I just wanted my marriage back. Recounting how much I wanted the separation but then how I caved in and everything was now wrong, I howled, "Tell me what to do!"

For a moment she was silent. Then she leaned forward and said, "This reaction sounds like fear of abandonment."

Fear of abandonment.

I had never heard those words before, but instinctively I knew that "fear of abandonment" summed up everything that had been wrong my whole life. And if there was a term for my condition, perhaps there was also a cure for it. I still wasn't sure of her, but I was willing to hear more. She gave me some books on trauma, abuse, codependency, and alcoholic family systems. Even though I was skeptical that these books held any answers, I promised to look at them.

Reading was painful, yet amazing. I had never read any self-help books before and had no idea that any would speak to what was broken in me. After being a foster child and an adoptee, I always felt like the odd person in every crowd—something my therapist would define as "terminal uniqueness." For the first time in my life, I felt hope and realized that I might actually be able to fix things I had thought were permanently broken.

It also never occurred to me that my husband was part of our problem. I was still operating under the assumption that everything wrong with our marriage was my fault. My therapist would later explain to me that "water seeks its own level" and that your partner's flaws and issues usually go hand in hand with your own. A person chooses a partner with a similar degree of "brokenness" and does a dance of dysfunction where they both know the steps. Therefore, one person cannot be so much healthier than the other. Healthy people do not dance with unhealthy people.

Still, I fervently believed that if I could find something in these books that resonated with my husband, I would connect with the man I loved, the father of my children, and bring him back to us.

So I would read the books and write him letters afterward. Sometimes he would get angry over a letter. Other times he would be sweet about it and we'd have long, dramatic talks that usually resulted in our falling into bed. Sometimes he'd come over and we'd both be confused and cry together. Other times we'd have screaming matches with name-calling and occasional violence. We were a mess, but every time we interacted, I hoped that whatever had happened would bring the separation to an end. I was still waiting for someone else to end my uncertainty.

Therapy was not helping to put my marriage back together. My therapist encouraged me to stop having contact with my husband except where the children were concerned. She encouraged me to journal and write letters to him that I would not send. She also encouraged me to look at my entire life and see all of the abuse, abandonment, and blame by others. If I wanted to stop the cycle of abuse and raise healthy children, I had to look at my entire life, figure out what had gone wrong, and fix it.

To do that, I had to go down into the abyss and face the pain.

The first month was the darkest time in my life, and I didn't think I was going to make it. Once the lid popped off, I realized I had opened an excruciatingly painful Pandora's box of loss and grief. It was hard to think that any good could come from such an agonizing task. To make matters worse, my husband was now being open about his relationship with a coworker, and I found a love letter from her in his car.

One day he came over to visit the boys when I was just getting in from work. I saw them playing in the backyard and went inside to change my shoes. The next thing I knew he was standing there, yelling at me for not saying hello. I didn't know how to respond. I sat there, still putting on my shoes and not answering him. He grew angrier, marched across the room, and slapped me in the face.

I didn't react, but quietly and firmly said, "Get out." The next day I saw a lawyer and finally filed for divorce and a restraining order. He wanted to challenge the restraining order, so we set a court date.

I knew he wanted the showdown-in-court date to intimidate me. He was probably thinking I would not go through with it, and the old me would not have. The only problem was that I *hadn't* ever stood up for myself and I wasn't sure I could do it. When the day came, as I walked up the courthouse steps, I was shaking and holding on to the railing to keep from falling over.

When our case was called, my lawyer put me on the stand and questioned me about the abuse, incident by incident. At first my voice was barely audible, but then I remembered my therapist's voice: *No one has the right to abuse another person.* I had never known that, always thinking that I made everyone do what they did because I was such a screwup.

As I repeated my therapist's words in my head like a mantra, something inside of me shifted. Deep down, I knew she had told me the truth. My entire persona changed; my voice grew stronger and louder. I turned and looked my husband in the eye.

To my astonishment, his lawyer whispered to him and then stood up to withdraw their objection to the restraining order. The judge said I could be seated and granted the permanent restraining order.

I practically floated down the stairs and out of the courthouse.

It was a new beginning. I knew that from that day forward, no one would ever abuse me again. I finally took control of my own life and said, "Enough! You cannot do this to me anymore!" Setting boundaries and limits became a priority in my life and changed everything for the better.

The divorce was not easy and took over two years to become final. But I kept working with my therapist, going to support groups, reading books, and getting stronger. Over the first holidays I had a bit of a relapse, but I leaned on my support system, moved past it, and kept doing the work.

All my life I had hated uncertainty and looked for someone to bring me security. All my life I had looked for someone to love me into being normal. Now I was learning that I had to make my own certainty, and discover and develop my own normalcy.

Even though it was hard, I not only confronted the past, but also changed my attitude in the present, and planned for the future.

I learned how to have friends, interests, and hobbies. As I spent time by myself discovering what I liked and what I didn't like, I was able to find my voice in relationships. The more I worked on myself and became healthier, the healthier the people in my life became.

The better I treated myself, the better I was treated. As my self-confidence grew, I met people who were loving and there for me when they said they would be.

With men, I learned how to date and how to say no. I learned to be true to myself and stopped trying to figure out what hoops I needed to jump through to get someone to like me. I started to ask myself, "Do I like him?" If I didn't, I said goodbye. Relationships weren't easy for me, and for the first few years my abandonment issues were in full force, but with each one I learned. When I started to see my relationships as learning experiences, and inventoried them when they were over, they helped me to understand what still needed attention in my life.

Along the way I decided what would have once been unthinkable: that I would rather be alone than accept the unacceptable from anyone. *Never again would I give up all that I am for a relationship.* I was not willing to be ignored, called names, or remain low on the priority list. I was not willing to accept unacceptable behavior just to keep someone around. For years I had been afraid that no one would love me. Now I was sure that I would get what I settled for, so I would not settle for less than I deserved. I was slowly coming to believe that I deserved the best.

It took a while for me to feel confident in my abilities as a parent. As I learned what was healthy and not healthy, it started to show in the kind of parent I became. We had boundaries in our house, cared about each other, and were there for each other. We didn't worry about stupid things like whether the counter was clean enough; we worried about being a family. Today my kids are grateful that I broke the cycle of abuse and abandonment. They never hang up the phone without saying they love me, and they always give me a hug when we greet and when we say goodbye. Whenever they need advice, they come to me. They are certain of me and I am certain of them. They are wonderful young men and I'm proud of them.

In trying to heal my broken places, I looked for my birth family. All through my abusive relationships, my heart cried for my brother Edward. I was certain that if he had been there, no harm would have come to me. Maybe I romanticized it, but to me he felt like my other half, lost somewhere in the world, and I wanted him in my life. I always thought that if we had been together, life would have been better for both of us.

It took me several years of searching to find him, and when I did I learned that Edward had died a few years earlier. I have two brothers, Billy and Ricky, and have forged relationships with them. My biggest grief has been not growing up with them and not being able to make that heal completely. I am as happy as I can be with a loss as big as never knowing my brother Edward and never being able to have a full history with my brothers. But other than that, I have healed the past. In therapy I worked through the relationships with all my parents, and I learned to accept them and eventually forgive them. I forgave them so that I could go on and heal.

Learning that "water seeks its own level," I was able to understand what issues needed attention by observing the people I was attracting and attracted to. It gave me the understanding that I could control what happened in my life and in my relationships. So many times I would think I was ready for "the one" and then get involved with someone with glaring issues. By looking at his issues, I was able to figure out what still needed work in my life and go back to the drawing board. Sometimes it was frustrating, but my goal was to improve myself to the point where I was ready and able to have a healthy relationship.

I was enjoying my single life when I met a man I fell in love with. He was a single parent as well, raising a little girl. He was honest, open, kind, and caring, and he thought I was the same. We both operated very well on our own, and each of us had decided we preferred to be alone rather than have any drama in our lives. The only way we would change that commitment to ourselves and our kids was if we found someone who lived life the same way. Neither of us thought we would, or could, find someone who valued our life and our kids, someone who encouraged independence and being who you are while forging a life together.

And then we found it in each other.

We've been happily married for over twelve years now. I can count our serious arguments on one hand. He has never called me a name. He has never made me cry. He doesn't care about the house's cleanliness; he cares about my happiness and loves me unconditionally. We are good and loving partners in life and in love.

Introduction

This book provides a clear plan for success after the end of a relationship. It is the culmination of my own experience as someone getting over a breakup, as a therapist, as an academic, and as a teacher. The material here is the core of how I turned the most devastating breakup into the best thing that ever happened to me—and how you can, too. It is all that I've learned in school and life, all that I've studied, and all that others have shared with me over the past twenty years.

After I ended my first marriage, I wanted to help people change their lives and tell them that anything was possible. I went to school to become a therapist and then a certified grief counselor through the Grief Recovery Institute. In doing research and leading grief groups, I saw the profound healing and positive effect that working through grief had on people. Whether it was from a breakup, a divorce, a death, or a sudden change, people who confronted their grief changed in amazing ways.

One day someone asked me if I had made all my dreams come true. I said I had, but the answer bothered me for days because there was one dream of mine that had not been fulfilled. As a child in the foster-care system, I thought about becoming a social worker or a lawyer when I grew up. The day of my final adoption in the Bronx County Courthouse, the judge brought me into his chambers to ask a few questions. Even as an eight-year-old, I was awestruck by the solemn, book-filled chamber and asked him how you get a job like this. The judge laughed and said, "Work hard, go to school, and become a lawyer." I silently vowed to do just that.

Thirty-two years after the conversation with the judge, I went to law school and, fulfilling my final dream, moved back to my hometown of New York City. Yet even though I was now immersed in legal practice every day, it seemed that, at the oddest times, someone would share with me their story of a breakup or someone they knew who was trying to leave an abusive situation. I would feel compelled to share my story, and each time I did, people encouraged me to keep telling it and helping others. Each time I tried to put it away, something would happen that would coax it back out, and someone would say I had to keep telling my story to give hope to others who were in similar situations.

To do that, I developed seminars called "Getting Past Your Past" (GPYP) and "Getting Past Your Breakup" (GPYB). I started a blog, an e-mail group, and a newsletter. I first started the blog to answer e-mail and questions from my seminar students. But after a few weeks, nonstudents began to comment on the entries. In just a short time, the blog developed a following and soon blog readers from all over the world were coming to seminars. GPYP blog readers have grown and developed into a wonderful support community; members talk privately and often travel together to seminars. New visitors to the blog are typically experiencing a lot of distress and are warmly welcomed into the community. The GPYP blog encourages longtime readers to "pay it forward," and they do. The community is a close and supportive resource for those hurting from a recent breakup.

My students and readers asked me for a book to lay out the road map to healing. So I compiled this book to share my journey and some of my knowledge. Mine was a very devastating breakup that was the catalyst for the wonderful life I have now—something I wish for everyone and fervently believe everyone can achieve.

This book, like the GPYP community, is all-inclusive for anyone experiencing a breakup: men or women, gay or straight, secular or spiritual, young or old. Grief is a universal emotion and there are concrete steps to move beyond it that apply to everyone. This book is for anyone who wants to know how to get over the loss of a relationship and move on to a full and happy life.

You Can Get Over This Relationship

Getting Past Your Breakup will help you forever change your relationships for the better. Unique to the plan is the concept of "observation, preparation, and cultivation." To change in a permanent way you need to observe what is going on in you and around you, prepare for change, and cultivate that change in your life. This book shows you how, every step of the way.

Most of the theories and techniques in this book come from classic and contemporary schools of psychological thought, but the *Getting Past Your Breakup* plan fits together in an original way.

From my own work and my work with others, I have learned that people tire of talk therapy and deep grief work with nothing fun, interesting, or self-soothing to balance it. On the other end of the spectrum, positive thinking and self-talk works well for a while, but it cannot work completely when there is great grief or pain stemming from childhood. While all of these theories and techniques have their place and do their job to some degree, this plan magnifies their effectiveness.

This book was not written to be read once and put away. It was written as a handbook so that you can revisit each chapter as often as you need to and use the book over the course of many months. It can be used in addition to and in conjunction with therapy and twelve-step programs or other support groups.

A healthy, happy life is one that is balanced. To get there, the steps you take must be balanced, too. It is important to use the tools here in relation to one another and to personalize it all to fit your own life.

The Getting Past Your Breakup plan works, and if you follow the advice in this book and work the program as laid out here, you will change your entire life. You will not only get over this latest breakup, you will become a person who is happy, healthy, and independent. And then you will attract others who are the same.

When you come face to face with your inner pain, do not retreat.

It hurts, but there is much goodness waiting for you.

Clear the wreckage of the past and find it.

Go down into the abyss and bring up the treasure that is your new life.

1

Road Map to Healing: How This Book Will Change Your Life

> The truth is that our finest moments are most likely to occur when we are feeling deeply uncomfortable, unhappy, or unfulfilled. For it is only in such moments, propelled by our discomfort, that we are likely to step out of our ruts and start searching for different ways or truer answers.
>
> M. SCOTT PECK

It's hard but it happens.

And it hurts.

You love someone who may have loved you once upon a time. Or who acted like there was a possibility of love in return, but now there's not. Or who simply doesn't feel the same way and isn't going to feel the same way.

Maybe your ex seemed to love you deeply, too. And then he or she just switched off and hurt you in ways that were unimaginable at the height of your mutual love.

Maybe someone new came along and your ex left. Friends tell you that you are better than this new person in every way. But your ex is still with Mr. or Ms. New Thing. You seethe because this new person is a snake in the grass and your ex doesn't see it. This new person is immature, unavailable, spoiled, or just plain stupid. And your ex is enthralled nonetheless. *What?*

Or maybe there is no one else and nothing else. Your ex just fell out of love one day. Or failed to fall in love on the day you did. That's even more baffling. Wait. You're choosing *nothing* over me? *What?*

Or maybe your ex has spiraled into some other mind-set. He or she is depressed, upset, self-absorbed in some way. *Don't you want someone to help carry the burden?* you ask. The answer you get is *Please leave me alone*. You're freaking out. How is it that he or she wants you to help by going away? *What?*

Maybe you initiated the breakup. Maybe your ex did. Whatever the situation, you're left with a big pile of hurt. And it *really* hurts. You go over your exchanges repeatedly in your mind. Where did it go wrong or fail to go right? What should you have done that you didn't? What did you do that you shouldn't have?

You feel rejected and "less than." You feel as if there is something really wrong with you. You wonder what you could do to *make* this person want you.

Stop right there.

Forget about changing *for someone else*. Forget about bargaining for what you should have without bribing whatever deity you believe in. Forget about losing yourself just so this narrow-minded person will love you. Forget it!

You deserve better—much better. And this book will show you how to get it.

While the aftermath of a breakup can be a devastating time, it can also be a tremendous opportunity for life-changing growth. As unbelievable as it may seem when you are in the throes of heartache, this can be a rich and fertile time when you are most open and ready to make your dreams come true. A breakup can actually be a liberating time when you take charge of your life and make positive change happen—instead of waiting around for it to happen to you.

During the post-breakup period, you have three options. The first is to spend all kinds of time, futile effort, and tears trying to win back your ex. The second is to try to go on as if nothing has happened and continue down the same path that led you into yet another unsuccessful relationship. The third option is to heal properly, look at what's happened, and learn new ways to put together a healthy and whole life. Not only will this make you happier, it will also give you the best chance to find true love with a person who is good *for* you and *to* you. Although the last option is infinitely more attractive and assures sustained long-term happiness, most people choose the first, and when that doesn't work, the second. Why? Because they have no idea how to do the third—to take charge of their lives.

Over the years I've met many clients, students, and readers who want meaningful change in their lives after a breakup but don't know how to make it happen. One woman said to me, "Since my divorce, I find myself at a crossroads in life, but I don't know which way to go." Another client of mine thought his divorce would be exhilarating, but then became frozen by indecision. He said, "There are so many things I've wanted to do but my ex-wife was a homebody, so I gave up so much. I want to do things now, but I'm still in pain from the breakup and the choices seem overwhelming."

When you are part of a couple, there is a certain rhythm of life combined with accountability to the relationship that precludes other choices. Once the relationship is over and those constraints no longer exist, you have a unique chance to assess your array of new options and decide what you want out of life, where you're going, and how you are going to get there. But being bewildered and afraid may keep you paralyzed.

Did you jump into your last relationship to escape something else? This opportunity you now have is not only about life choices but also about your emotional condition. After a breakup, many people who seek therapy or go to support groups discover that there are parts of themselves that have been unhealed for a very long time. One woman told me, "I stuffed all of my bad memories from previous abuse while I was with my boyfriend. The minute the relationship ended, the memories returned. I could not outrun my pain." Another man sought counseling after his marriage broke up and was surprised to find his therapist focusing on his mother's death when he was a young boy. He said:

> I've never been able to handle loss, and when my wife left, I was so depressed I thought I was going to die. But it wasn't about my wife. It was about experiencing my mother's death all over again. I was too young to grieve her, so I didn't. Later I became clingy and whiny in relationships and tried to avoid any loss at

all. When my wife left, I had to go back and finally grieve my mother's death.

Perhaps you have had smaller losses, a move or a job change, that you've never fully recognized as something to grieve. Perhaps you have never really experienced a significant loss and this breakup is a first for you. Whether you have unresolved grief or not, learning to work through loss is one of the most healthy things you can do.

Emotional pain has an upside—it can motivate you to examine certain aspects of your life in a way that doesn't happen when you are comfortable. The new breakup pain coupled with old, unresolved grief can bring you to a place where you can address issues and recover—in a way you're not able to do when you're not facing a major loss.

Opportunity plus willingness means that this breakup is the *best* time to change your life for the better, inside and out. Unfortunately, few people take the opportunity because after the first blush of freedom, the reality of being alone begins to overshadow the promise of change. The emotional pain becomes so great that willingness to work through it is replaced with a drive to "feel better" and put everything in the past. Even if you have every intention of getting past the breakup, both emotionally and logistically, it may seem like an impossible task because life alone seems scary and unclear.

One man shared in my seminar, "We operated as a couple for so long that I don't know who I am right now." Another woman said, "I want to do so many things, but I don't know how to get through this and exist on my own. Some days I have trouble leaving the house. I'm afraid of picking somebody, anybody, just so I'm not alone."

Your insecurities may take over; you may feel unattractive or dread that you will be alone the rest of your life. You may begin to doubt the soundness of your decisions and plans. Maybe you've always wanted to go back to school, take up a new hobby, or move somewhere else, but suddenly this feels self-indulgent and ridiculous. Your self-esteem may plummet as you become immobilized by indecision. You may backpedal on your plans for a new life because it's terrifying to venture forth to unfamiliar places. The push to a new relationship or the pull back to the old one—or just sitting and waiting until something comes along—may begin to take hold.

Getting into another relationship or losing your resolve to change your life is not going to make anything better—it's just a temporary panacea. In fact, a new relationship will probably be like the last one because you haven't learned anything, nor have you worked through the pain of the breakup. Putting your hopes and dreams on hold will not extinguish them; it will just fill you with regret at the end of the next relationship that you didn't get going on them sooner.

Right now, the best thing to do is to meet this challenge head on, work through your grief, make those plans, and change your life. So how do you do that when you're overcome by grief, fear of the future, and practical everyday matters?

If you think it's very hard to do without direction, you're absolutely right. The post-breakup terrain is very difficult to maneuver without a guide, and this is why people report feeling indecisive, scared, and ready to rush into another relationship.

Getting Past Your Breakup is your much-needed road map through the process. It will help you keep your determination, make changes, and do things differently from now on by teaching you, step-by-step, how to face the loss, assess the past, plan for the future, and turn the present into a positive and pleasant experience. You'll discover how to have new, healthy relationships and how to thrive when you're single, either temporarily or as a permanent choice. You don't have to figure it all out by yourself any longer! Now you have a dependable route to your new and happy life.

The Road Map to Healing

What is the path from loss and sorrow to healing and happiness? How do you get from the first horrifying moments of Point A to the cheery and welcoming place of Point B?

You get there after you learn how to put yourself first and nurture yourself while allowing the spectrum of emotions to be felt. You get there after you work on the past, while valuing yourself in the present, all while planning for the future. That is how it happens.

There are a few things to keep in mind as you travel on the path. The first is simply this: Nature abhors a vacuum. This means that if you take something, or someone, out of your life, something else will come along to replace it. The problem is that this new thing might not be something you welcome. Think back on times you tried to break a bad habit and became so focused on "stopping" that you didn't realize you had unconsciously picked up some other unhealthy habit! To avoid that, you need to exert some control over what replaces that which has gone out of your life. As you work out hurt and anger, you have to replace it with a positive self-image, positive goals, new interests, and being good to yourself. The process works when you let out the emotions of grief as you let in a new self-image, new things to do, and new plans and goals.

Everything must be brought into balance: your emotional state, your thinking state, your behavior, and your interaction with the world. Every day you will work out the pain and work in the good. Each day you will affirm yourself, commit to the process, work through the difficult feelings, and plan for the future while following key practical guidelines.

To be successful during this breakup, there are certain things you must do. The first thing is to learn to *observe, prepare,* and *cultivate.* You'll use these skills over and over again. Through observation, you will learn what is really happening in your life internally and externally. You will learn to respond, and not react. By preparing, you will learn how to be ready for many different things that come along. Finally, cultivation will keep your new changes working in your life day after day.

To grow and change, you must acknowledge and express your feelings of hurt, anger, confusion, anxiety, and frustration. You must affirm yourself and think about you in a positive way. You must put your goals on paper. You must review your relationship and your role in it. You must get out and meet new people as well as spend productive time alone. This back-and-forth must be done every single day. All along the way, *Getting Past Your Breakup* will remind you to keep the balance.

The Main Destinations: Taking Care of Yourself, Working Out the Grief, and Dealing with Challenges

The path to healing has three main destinations:

Taking Care of Yourself

Working Out the Grief

Dealing with Challenges

By understanding and balancing these three things, you are on the road to happiness and wholeness.

Taking Care of Yourself. Starting today, put yourself first. Self-care is so important because it gives you the fortitude and resiliency to deal with your present painful feelings and revisit difficult times long ago. You need inner strength to do the work required, and this strength comes from boosting your self-esteem by affirming yourself with kind, loving, and positive thoughts; doing nice things for yourself each week; and developing your goals, interests, hobbies, and networks of friends while avoiding self-destructive behaviors. By attending to your well-being, you will be stronger and more focused as you work through the moving-on process. You will find a rhythm that not only works as you get over this relationship, but that stays with you the rest of your life.

Taking care of yourself should start right away, so in Chapter 4 you'll learn how to immediately begin incorporating being good to yourself into your daily life. You'll want to reread this chapter often so that you develop the habit of taking care of yourself every day. In this chapter you will learn how to journal, write affirmations and gratitude lists, retrain your brain away from obsessive thinking, take frequent breaks, set goals, set aside a special night each week for yourself, and build support systems.

After you've done the bulk of your grief work in the middle chapters, you will emerge a happier person and ready to take your self-care to another level in Chapter 7, where you'll learn how to take care of yourself in relationships. Developing boundaries is probably the most productive thing you can do to ensure a healthy and happy life because boundaries are the key to all loving relationships.

In Chapter 8, you'll learn how to have the best life possible, whether partnered or single. You'll be able to decide whether you want another relationship and, if so, what you want from that relationship. You will discover how to find the joy (yes, joy!) in being single so that you are never so dependent on a relationship that you settle for less than you deserve.

And, importantly, you will also learn how to reengage the world of dating and relationships—especially how to approach and survive those first post-breakup dates. You'll know how not to take rejection personally, and how to shift your focus from worrying about what someone else thinks of you to objectively deciding whether this is a person you want to spend more time with. As you get ready for a new relationship, you'll be able to recognize what real love and healthy relationships look like, and know how to stay true to yourself while making a relationship work.

Working Out the Grief. This is the centerpiece of the book, and it is in these middle chapters that you'll work out your feelings of loss by looking not only at your last relationship but also at your relationship patterns. Chapter 3 explains the process of grief and how to cope with each phase as well as how to know that you are nearing the end of the process.

After a breakup you may feel numb for a time, and then reality hits hard. When the feelings of loss and grief start to surface, you may be inclined to hide from them. You may try to avoid the pain through unhealthy behaviors—drugs, alcohol, food, sex, shopping, rebound relationships, workaholism, isolation, nonstop activity, reconnecting with your ex—any number of avoidance behaviors. Or you may try to suppress it altogether and return to your life as if nothing happened. But the pain of not acknowledging the loss will eat you up inside or come out sideways, ruining another relationship down the road. Not dealing with this breakup might seem to make sense in the short term, but it will just add to your long-term misery.

You're probably already experiencing some of this. There may be past losses you've been afraid to face, and the pain of this new loss has opened the floodgates, allowing old losses to rush to the surface and compound the pain. If you suppress these feelings yet again, it will happen again somewhere down the line, with the mountain of suppressed feelings getting bigger and bigger. But if you stop now to face your pain, you will mend and be happy, no longer on the run from past hurt. In Chapter 6, you will learn how to examine not only your last relationship but all of the relationships in your life. The most important piece of work you will do to get beyond this breakup is taking the Relationship Inventory. After that, you'll move onto an equally important piece of work to prepare for your next relationship, the Life Inventory.

The Relationship Inventory is designed to give you a realistic view of the relationship. It will help you to avoid fantasizing about how great it was, or being so focused on how horrible it was that you don't do your grief work. In writing the Relationship Inventory, you'll learn to step back and look at the relationship with a critical eye.

While the Relationship Inventory is about doing your grief work and learning from the relationship you just ended, the Life Inventory is about restructuring how you relate to other people: You will learn how to go back and take care of unfinished business, and how to deal with unresolved grief that existed before your last relationship. This part of the work involves looking at you and only you.

In the Life Inventory you will look at all your former partners as well as your relationships with parents, siblings, and other caretakers to see how these primary relationships are still affecting your choices. You will do a Parent Inventory that you can also apply to other important caretakers. This work will be ongoing and serve as a structure for your self-assessment in the future. Whenever you are uncertain or confused about what is going on in a relationship, you'll be able to look at your Life Inventory and figure it out.

The final working-it-out chapter is Chapter 9, "Letters from Readers and Frequently Asked Questions." The Q & A chapter has actual e-mails and messages from readers of the "Getting Past Your Past" blog. Here you will find common concerns, questions, thoughts, and feelings similar to your own and learn how best to deal with them.

Dealing with Challenges. The last area covers practical advice to help with daily challenges and common pitfalls. These chapters serve as guides for when you are feeling emotionally low, and for when you are vulnerable to falling into traps that keep you stuck and threaten your healing process.

Inevitably, there are two problem areas after a breakup: communication with your ex and, if you are a parent, dealing with your children. Chapters 2 and 5 give down-to-earth, practical advice that you can follow to make these thorny issues less difficult. These chapters should be read again and again until following the advice becomes second nature.

Chapter 2 is devoted to the hardest thing: not being in touch with your ex. You need to separate emotionally, physically, and psychologically from the relationship, and the biggest mistake that will hinder that separation is continued contact. Most people struggle with the urge to connect and fool themselves into thinking it is okay to get in touch for certain reasons. This chapter dismantles the classic excuses for staying in touch with your ex and teaches you that while going "no contact" is difficult, the rewards are many. This chapter helps you commit to "no contact" without excuses.

Chapter 5 is another practical chapter and is designed for newly single parents. Raising children is exhausting under optimal circumstances, but after a breakup it can be extremely challenging. This chapter gives straight advice on how to cope with the children and help them cope with the breakup. Not only is this good, practical advice for the immediate aftermath of a breakup, but it will also teach you to be a better parent wherever the future takes you and your children.

The Life and Love You Want *Is* Achievable

Part of this book is about healing your losses. Several of my clients, students, and readers have come to realize that they spent all their adult lives in relationships in which they were only running from grief. One woman's fear of loss was so chronic that, from the time she was a teenager, she never left a relationship until she had started a new one. She said, "I thought I would die if I had to be alone, so I kept going from one man to another without a single day alone." When she was in her thirties, a man she had been seeing for a few years suddenly left her and she didn't have a new relationship on the horizon. The breakup was traumatic, and she fell apart because she finally had to grieve all the relationships she had never grieved before. It was a distressing time, but once she worked through her losses and found the strength and courage to put together a new life, she was surprised to find that being on her own was wonderful. Grieving her relationships not only didn't kill her, but set her free in a way she never could have predicted during those years spent running from one relationship to another.

Once you've worked through a significant loss, you come out on the other side unafraid, and when you're not afraid, you make better choices. And when you make better choices, you have happier relationships with healthy people. Doing your grief work is the secret to living fully and loving freely.

The second part of *Getting Past Your Breakup* teaches you to use this breakup as a catalyst to transform your life into everything you've always wanted it to be. Many of my clients, students, and readers have used their breakups to bring great change to their lives. One man realized about a year after his breakup, that his life was not just taking shape, but it was turning into something he never dreamed possible before the relationship ended. He grieved the loss of his relationship and worked hard to change his negative self-image. By building support networks, finding new interests, and setting goals, he found that he had not only gotten past his breakup but was, in many ways, very grateful that it had happened!

Another woman agrees:

> I don't know when it clicked, but it did. For months I cried and walked the floor. I had night phobias and no confidence. But I wrote in my journal, worked on my self-esteem, and learned to be good to myself. I found creative things to do with new and interesting people. All along I thought I was just "keeping busy" but found that I was actually, unwittingly, building the life I've always wanted. The breakup was the best thing that ever happened to me.

And so it can be for you, too. If you've never taken chances, you can now take them. If you've only dreamed about the life you've wanted, you can now put things in place to have it. You can use this time to come to grips with finally walking through the pain and getting over it, once and for all. You can use this time to learn about you and what you want, to learn how to be good to yourself so that you will insist, in the future, that others treat you well. You can use this time to discover how to have true love and true intimacy, and how to forgo the unhealthy attachments of the past. You can take this opportunity to find out how to make good and healthy choices, to turn the page and build a life you may not have ever thought possible.

Following this road map will heal the hurt while building your self-esteem and teaching you how to make your dreams a reality.

It will put you in charge of your life again and help you move on to things that are bigger and better than you've ever dreamed possible. And you will live the life you were meant to live. This is the road map that will turn your devastating breakup into the best thing that ever happened to you. So follow it, do the work, heal the hurt, and build a life that is second to none.

2

The Rules of Disengagement: Going "No Contact" with Your Ex

> The patient says, "Doctor, it hurts when I do this."
> The doctor says, "Then don't do that!"
>
> HENNY YOUNGMAN

When my marriage ended, there were no cell phones and my ex didn't have e-mail or even an answering machine. It was almost impossible to stay in touch . . . but I did everything I could think of to send messages to him. I would call incessantly and hang up when he answered (or worse, when the new girlfriend answered). I would write long, rambling letters and then wait for him to come by and get them. When he didn't, I would drive to where he worked and stick them under the windshield wipers of his car. It was crazy and compulsive behavior that I couldn't seem to stop, but, incredibly, I didn't think I was connecting with him all that much.

When my therapist insisted that I keep a log of every time I contacted my ex or answered his communications, then it was there, in black and white—I just wasn't letting go. I had to force myself to end the contact, to walk away and not be available for a phone call or a visit. I had to put boundaries in place and not allow him to just move in and out of my life. It was tough in the beginning, and it felt just like breaking an addiction. But to my surprise, I noticed that when I started to decrease my communication with him, I started to feel better.

Today if I had to pinpoint one issue that is almost universal among people who struggle with their breakups, it's that they cannot or will not stop communicating. Over the years I've counseled many people who have enormous difficulty staying away from their exes. I've heard endless reasons people stay in touch, from "I think we could be friends" to "I want to be available in case a reconciliation is possible."

Yet even when a relationship is truly over, people still have trouble ending contact. In order to truly get past your breakup, you need to separate emotionally, physically, and psychologically from the relationship, and the primary way to do that is to stop talking to your ex. Therefore, ending communication is a priority because it will give you enough space to find peace, allow you to heal, and help you move on.

In general, it is best to cut off all forms of communication, to go "no contact" (what we call NC). Today it's incredibly easy to reach out and touch someone—too easy. Therefore, it's important that you make the decision that you're not going to call, e-mail, text, or leave voice-mail messages, and you're not going to answer if your ex decides it's time to talk. You must commit to NC, and then do your best to keep that commitment no matter what happens.

Cutting off all communication is difficult to do, especially in the beginning. You used to spend a great deal of time together and were most likely the biggest part of each other's lives. Now there is a terrible void, and you want to reach out and fill it with the comfort of the person you've just broken up with. A quick "hello" might seem innocent enough and you're convinced you can keep it light, but you're only fooling yourself. If you reach out, you stall the moving-on process. You can't find the new when you're holding on to the old, so you need to just let go.

After a person goes NC, he or she typically experiences some difficulty at first but then the benefits kick in. One woman said to me:

> NC is going well at last. In the past forty-eight hours rather than feeling I can't breathe without him, it feels like I can breathe better without him! I had a little cry yesterday, but the tears were nothing compared to what they would have been if I had contacted him and got the response I've been getting. He's been angry and upset, and each call made me feel worse than the last one. I think at long last I am beginning to realize that I really am a strong, independent woman who does not need an ex-lover to complicate her life!

A man who struggled with NC and characterized himself as "the one who calls endlessly" finally was able to stop. He reported: "I took her number off my phone, and her e-mail address is no longer in my address book. I haven't talked to her in two weeks and am slowly getting back to normal." Another man said to me:

> I broke up with my girlfriend a few months ago after she suddenly decided the relationship was over. I made the mistake of e-mailing a few days later and got a long response about why she broke up with me. Then I called her, we had an argument, and she hung up on me. After that I kept writing and calling to apologize, but she wouldn't answer me. I realized that I had to stop. At first it was very hard, but it's been a few weeks and I'm feeling better. Going NC has helped me immensely.

It may seem most challenging to keep this commitment when you're feeling down and upset. There may be moments when you miss your ex so much you can't stand it a minute longer and feel you simply must get in touch! But I can't stress this enough—you simply mustn't.

This urge is normal and natural and will pass if you learn to sit with it or do other things instead of picking up the phone or tapping out a note on the computer. Grief is a hard process, and it may seem that contact will temporarily alleviate the pain. But it doesn't alleviate it; it just postpones the inevitable. Eventually you're going to have to deal with how you really feel.

You may understand, intellectually, that you shouldn't be in contact, but then you think of a hundred different reasons you need to talk. Well, put aside the reasons, because they're not really reasons: They are excuses, and everyone has one or two favorites that stand in the way of moving on.

As a therapist, I heard a lot of excuses clients give for absolutely having to be in touch. Since I started GPYP and my blog, I've heard even more. But I've found that the reasons always seem to fit into one of seven categories. The stories vary from person to person, but the excuse is really the same.

I spend a lot of time helping people to understand why these reasons are just excuses, and why they need to stop using them and move on. I want you to stop using them and move on as well. If you're really creative, you'll come up with different excuses than the ones listed below, but these are the most common. Even if your excuse isn't on the list, the advice following the seven excuses probably fits your situation as well. Using these excuses will just keep you going back for more, making it harder to do your work and impossible to transition to your new and wonderful life. So stop using them!

The Seven Excuses That Will Keep You Stuck

1. "Why can't we be friends?"

"Even though my relationship with my girlfriend didn't work out, we still call and text each other all the time, trying to be friends. It's not working but I'm not sure why. We're arguing more than we did during our relationship."

"My boyfriend broke up with me and moved in with another woman. He keeps writing and calling me, telling me that we were meant to be good friends and he doesn't want to lose me completely. I am heartbroken and have difficulty every time I see him. When I say I'm not ready, he says it's time to forgive and forget. He's offered to give me time, but I'm not sure I can get there anytime soon. He says I'm being unreasonable. Am I wrong to refuse his offers of friendship?"

"My ex walks by me and says hello like it's the most natural thing in the world. Once he asked me out to lunch and I thought it was to reconcile, but he only said he hoped we could be friends. I really don't want to be friends with him."

The variations on this theme are many. Even if your ex doesn't come right out and say, "Can't we be friends?" you might sense an inability to let go and let you be. You might initially be flattered that he or she can't imagine life without you, but, honestly, it usually has more to do with your ex's inability to end things than a true desire to keep you around.

While there are many versions of "let's be friends" and your mileage may vary, the advice remains the same: Trying to be friends with your ex is a losing strategy most of the time. Even if the breakup was amicable, the people involved need some time to work through their feelings and sift through the ruins of the relationship. Even if the breakup was not dramatic and chaotic—even if the breakup was downright friendly—there needs to be time apart to break the bond of the couple.

After a breakup, the work each person has to do is to lose the couple identity. In other words, each person needs to establish his or her individual identity, and no longer see him or herself as part of the couple they once were. Depending on the length of the relationship, there may be a part of you that sees you as "John and Mary"—not just John and not just Mary. There are automatic daily motions that define the groove of a couple and, for a while, you're still in them. You may see something you would normally pick up at the store for your ex, or you might stop to call at the same time you used to call every day. There is a part of you that connects certain places, times, and events to your ex. To break this connection, you need to take some time and have no contact.

Some couples manage to become friends later, but if that is ever to be, it should be much later. Immediately following a breakup, the atmosphere is too emotionally charged for this to happen right away, if at all. You both need time to get yourselves together. If you leave each other alone initially, you may come back later as saner, more grounded people with a better chance of being friends. But right now you need to concentrate on yourself and your healing.

It's also hard to be friends because ex-lovers don't hold each other to the same standard as they do other friends. There is a gray area of uncharted territory due to unfinished business, sore subjects, and off-limits discussions. It's difficult to tease or joke around, and certain words can be taken the wrong way. You might think you can do it without a problem, but the skin is thinner and the chance for upheaval, or even crisis, is greater. It's not a "true" friendship and usually can't be treated as one no matter how hard you try. There is always the unspoken "stuff" and unresolved issues that stand in the way.

The person who pushes to "be friends" is usually the one who doesn't want the commitment or responsibility of the relationship but is unwilling to completely relinquish the companionship of someone familiar. Of course, there are things that you liked about this person. If there weren't, you would have never been together. Everyone misses some trait of their ex's at some point, but this doesn't mean it makes sense to keep someone around just for that, all the while putting up with things you don't like at all.

On the other hand, there are also reasons you're no longer together, and perhaps those are the same reasons you shouldn't be friends. One woman broke up with a man who was controlling and critical. After it ended, he wanted to be friends and she was uncomfortable with that. True to form, he told her that she was weak and insecure if she couldn't figure out how to be friends. She kept him in her life for a while to prove him wrong, but finally came to realize that, as she put it, "an ex is an ex for a reason." She ended the friendship for the same reasons she ended the relationship.

If you're the one who is asking to be friends, examine your motives. Are you trying to avoid feeling loss and grief? Are you playing a game? Are you unwilling to break all ties even though you don't want the relationship? Are you expecting to have all the "benefits" of this person without any corresponding responsibility?

If you're the person who is being asked to be friends, say no. If your ex is saying that he or she simply can't be without you because you're such a wonderful person, ask yourself this: Were you truly valued when you were together? Face it, your friends should treat you well, and if your ex has mistreated you, why would you want to count this person as a friend? Regardless of explanations and justifications, examine your ex's behavior and ask yourself: Can you ever really trust a friend who would behave this badly toward you?

Another consideration is how to push back on your ex's reassurances that being friends is the answer for both of you. One man says:

> My girlfriend of five years told me a few days ago that she doesn't love me anymore but wants us to be close minus the romance. I don't want to stay away from her, but I can't escape the pain when I'm with her. I know things are not the same and that I've lost part of her. She insists I've not lost her; it's just that my status in her life has changed. I'm insecure and constantly wonder what will happen when she decides to date. I'm worried I'll turn into a possessive and suspicious friend. I don't want to just be her friend, but I don't know how to tell her when she is so sure it will work out fine.

Another woman bemoans the fact that her ex doesn't understand her reluctance to be friends. "We were friends," she says, "and then we were lovers. He doesn't think being lovers is working, and we should just forget it ever happened and go back to being friends. I still have very strong feelings for him and don't know if I can."

Being in a relationship or friendship is a two-way decision. Just because your ex wants to remain friends doesn't mean you have to, especially if your ex is the one who broke it off. The two of you are in different positions and have different sensitivities. While it may be easy for your ex, it may not be easy for you. You need to take care of yourself, and you don't need anyone's approval to make a decision. You have the right to say no. Short and sweet. Pure and simple. No.

Your ex might have an issue with your rebuff and may try to convince you that you're not being nice, fair, or mature. But this is not about being nice, fair, or mature, so don't fall into any traps where you will be manipulated into arguing the point! Don't try to explain or rationalize. If you're really feeling pressure, you might want to try, "No, not now." However, if you're sure, the best thing to do is to say no and not invite discussion. You're much better off staying apart.

Draw a boundary and insist that you get your space.

Then take it.

And bask in it.

2. "I must have closure."

"I asked my ex if he ever loved me. He wouldn't answer me. I need to know this to get closure and move on."

"My ex asked me for a break in the relationship six months ago. Now she doesn't know if she's ever coming back. I've asked if we can meet so that if it's over, I can have closure. She doesn't really want to meet with me and I don't know what to do to get closure."

"I keep calling my ex to try to understand what happened and get closure, but I am never satisfied with the answers."

I've had countless clients and readers say to me, "I need closure," truly believing that to get closure, they need to say things to or ask things of their exes. But insisting upon closure is really just an excuse to reconnect.

As a grief therapist I have counseled many people after a large variety of circumstances, including sudden death and suicide of a loved one. These families are devastated. They are stricken with a loss, and they have many questions. Even if they may never know all the answers, they still are able to find closure. You don't need answers or explanations to find closure. No matter what the loss, the closure comes from inside you.

You may have many questions, but you need to accept that some will never be answered. Even if you have questions that seem to drive you crazy, you must decide that the answers don't matter, probably won't make sense, probably aren't going to satisfy you, and are not going to give you a sense of closure. It is your responsibility to accept that you may have to close this chapter without answers, without explanations, and without input from someone else. It is not only possible for you to survive without the answers, but it's necessary. Staying in the questions, repeating them, and ruminating over the possible answers will only keep you stuck.

Despite your fervent belief that somehow having one final scene with your ex will lead to closure, it will not. You don't need to know what your ex thinks, or why your ex did this or that to move on. If you want closure, you need to do your grief work, integrate the experience into your life, and turn the page. That is how closure happens.

Another possibility is that the quest for closure may actually make you feel worse. The ex could choose to ignore you completely. One woman wrote, "I decided to go NC but planned on sending a 'goodbye and thanks for all the memories' closure e-mail. I told myself that I expected no reply, but I know that when I don't get one I will be crushed. That will do me no good, so I've decided against the closure e-mail."

Another possibility is that your ex may use your contact as an excuse to castigate you. A blog reader lamented the fact that her attempt at closure led to a nasty conversation with her ex. She wrote:

> Every time I attempted to contact him to gain some closure, he ignored me. Finally, he responded to a letter by blaming me for everything and accusing me of things that weren't true. He made up things about what had happened. I know he'll never give me closure or acknowledge how wrong he was for any of this. This has been difficult to accept, but I know now that [going "no contact"] is what I must do.

As difficult as it is, at some point you have to accept that "it is what it is" and you may never understand exactly what that is. You need to accept that you don't have all the answers, that you never will have all the answers, and that you never will get to say everything you want to say. But you need to move on anyway. And you will.

3. "I just need to make sense of it all" and "I just have one more thing to say to you before I go."

> "For three years my ex-boyfriend said he loved me and I was the only person for him. I was fearful about getting involved and being hurt, but he swept me off my feet. He talked about marriage and children, and we even looked at a few places to have a wedding. When I was completely committed, he suddenly reversed course and broke off the relationship. The things he said go round and round in my head and I keep trying to talk to him to make sense of what he said and then what he did."

"My girlfriend was a very sensible person who loved me and said I was the best thing that ever happened to her. About six months ago she started acting strangely. She started to stay out late and party with unruly people. She dropped out of college and started working in a seedy place. She then broke up with me. I have spent the past few months trying to understand what is wrong with her and why she took this sudden turn. She won't answer my calls and I need to understand what happened."

"My husband of twenty-five years just moved out one day after he met someone else. I'm devastated and want him to explain how he could throw our lives away like that."

"My wife went on a business trip and hooked up with this coworker she always said she couldn't stand. I had to move out of the house and it kills me to not see my kids every day. I don't get how she could say she was so happy in our marriage and then just divorce me for someone she claimed to have despised. I ask her to explain this to me all the time and she won't. I believe she owes me an explanation."

"I broke up with my boyfriend and he took it very hard. He keeps calling me and telling me all these things that I did wrong in the relationship. No matter how much I defend myself, he won't listen to the truth. He accuses me of trying to hurt him and cheating on him. I never did any such thing. He has exaggerated everything that ever happened between us. I don't know how to make him believe that I did not do all these things. He keeps saying he will stop calling and then he calls

> and says, 'I have one more thing I have to say. ' I keep defending myself but I'm tired of it. He thinks of me as such a bad person and I want to make him see that I'm not, I just needed to get out of the relationship."

> "My girlfriend broke up with me and yet keeps calling and writing to tell me all the things that are wrong with me. I'm hurt enough by the breakup and I just want her to leave me alone, but she says I owe it to her to hear her out. I listen to her and don't respond, but later I think about all the things she said and how wrong she is about me and I call her to set the record straight."

It may be tempting to question your ex so that you can understand what went wrong when. You may not know how you started drifting apart or why that last silly argument led to "It's over." You may be convinced you did nothing wrong and you are meant to be together. This all seems unnecessary, and thinking back on the relationship just makes you more perplexed. You were told you were the best thing ever. You were so loved. You both agreed you were perfect together. Then it was over. Your head reels with incomprehension. How could this be? How could this person say "I love you" one day and "I don't want to be with you anymore" the next? What's really going on? Is it something different from what he or she is saying? How is this breakup a good thing?

You may think that if you can just talk some sense into your ex, then everything will be fine. You may have heard illogical or unreasonable explanations that left you stunned and speechless at the time, but now they go round and round in your head and you can think of a thousand rebuttals to them all. As you ruminate on the things your ex said, you come up with all the reasons your ex is wrong, and then you start to imagine how having a chance to talk things out will resolve all the misunderstandings. It becomes your impassioned belief that you can have a conversation and turn this wrongheadedness around.

If your ex dumped you and you think it was the wrong thing to do, he or she needs to figure that out. You can't be the one to "fix" your ex's thinking. The bottom line is that if your ex sees things in a cockeyed way now, he or she is going to continue to see things the same way whenever you're not around to correct this twisted perspective. It takes hard work and constant vigilance to keep someone "thinking correctly," and you don't want that kind of responsibility or control. The fact is, you need to accept that you have been with someone whose approach to life is simply incompatible with yours. Perhaps it was always evident that you thought in different ways, saw the world differently, and operated on irreconcilable levels, but you chose to ignore it or worked hard to correct it. You can't ignore the dissimilar viewpoints any longer. Accept the fact that you think differently and let it go so you can find someone whose way of thinking is compatible with yours.

Sometimes, instead of trying to talk, people continue to contact each other to continue the angry arguments that led to the breakup in the first place. While it may be tempting to scream your head off at someone who has hurt you, again, it's best to avoid it. If your ex decides to tell you everything that is wrong with you (which often happens on a continuing basis), shut it down. You do not need to hear, continually, what is wrong with you or to explain to anyone what is not wrong with you. Similarly, you don't need to say every "one last thing" that you would like to say. Instead, if you have a million thoughts going through your head, you can try writing down everything you would ever want to say in a letter that you never send.

It hurts when someone who once loved you insists on revisiting the relationship and discussing who did what to whom. Often these conversations will center around your faults or assign attributes to you that are not true. It's easy to get defensive and sucked into arguments. Don't. The better way to handle it is to let your ex think whatever your ex wants to think. If you are being blamed for everything that went wrong, cultivate an attitude of, "Who cares?" Even if you do care and these barbs hurt, keep telling yourself that what your ex or your ex's family or friends think of you is none of your business. Use this as a mantra that you say over and over again.

It's important that you stop your side of the argument as well. Don't ask for justifications for present or past behavior, or say how much you've been hurt. Yes, there are things you want this person to think about, but it's not healthy for you to expend energy trying to convince someone who refuses to be convinced. Save yourself the trouble. Everyone will be happier in the end. If you let go of this person and your need to control or condemn, you will be free to find someone whose thinking is compatible with yours. As long as you hold on to this "wrongheaded" person, you will not find the person who is "rightheaded" enough for you. Let it go and save your energy for building your new life.

4. "I want to be available for reconciliation."

"I have tried to keep in contact with my ex with a view to salvaging our broken relationship. Although I was aware she had met someone else, I conveniently ignored this and kept the communication channels open."

"I have stayed in communication with my ex to remain in a holding pattern—waiting until she wants me back again. I thought there was no sense in grieving if we are getting back together. I couldn't admit my fear that if I stopped contacting her, I would ruin all chances of her coming back."

"I wanted to prove my love to him by staying close and letting him know I was there for him. I called it a lot of different things—trying to be a friend, seeking closure, looking for answers—but it was a veiled attempt at trying to win him back."

Sometimes people don't acknowledge that they are staying in touch to keep the hope of reconciliation alive. One man said, "I thought I was being a friend but was in denial that I was just trying to prove to her that I was worth keeping." Another woman said, "I made every excuse in the book for staying in touch with him because I could not admit that the real reason was to get back together." Examining your quest for contact and being honest about your real intentions will help you stop making excuses to make contact. Even if it is your fervent hope that you will reconcile, taking a break and going NC will help you regardless of what happens down the line.

You both have been through a trying time, and you must face that a break will do each of you a world of good. Now is the time to reassess where you've been and where you're going, even if you're going there together. You still need to take stock of yourself and the relationship so that you can figure out what went wrong and what needs to go right in the future. Until the communication ends, it is impossible to do that. Even if you do reconcile, the relationship you once knew has ended, so you must grieve the relationship that has passed and move on from what once was. Because if you do reconcile, it has to be different than it was before, or it will just fail. Again.

5. "I just need to give this stuff back."

People become very creative in finding ways to stay in touch with their exes. One of the most "innocent" ploys I've found is when one person insists on retrieving something—a piece of clothing, a household item—that belongs to him or her. A former client of mine once went back for a plastic bowl, showing up unannounced and interrupting her ex and his new girlfriend in the middle of a Sunday afternoon. She went there under the guise of really needing it for a cookout she was having. She was probably the last person he wanted to see on that particular day, but he looked for the bowl anyway. Unable to find it, he said he would look for it another time and send it to her. She refused to leave, carrying on and causing such a scene that the neighbors called the police. The fuss, she said, was because he could not locate the bowl. Hmmm, do you really think that's what it was all about?

Before you are taken away in handcuffs, think about how important the item really is. If you need to return it, put it in a box and mail it. No note, no nothing. If you are the one who wants it, think about it: Is it worth more than your sanity? Probably not.

There should be an initial exchange of belongings within days after a breakup. If you need help arranging to pick up your things, get it right away. Don't let it drag on and on. No one is responsible for another person's things forever. After a reasonable time (a few weeks), a person is legally free to discard someone else's belongings if that person has not made an effort to retrieve them. So get your things back within a short time of the breakup.

Do not ask for gifts back or take gifts back. Gifts are gifts—they belong to the person who received them. One important exception is the engagement ring. If you're a woman who was given an engagement ring and your ex paid for it, it's best not to keep it. An engagement ring is not a gift; it is given in contemplation of marriage. Even if the ring was given on your birthday or a holiday, it is not a gift. If the marriage does not happen, you should give the engagement ring back sooner rather than later.

Making a clean break is important, so clear up loose ends immediately. Avoid keeping anything or leaving anything that can be asked for later on. If you still have things, return them. If there are things you've left behind, ask for them once more. Otherwise forget it, and move on.

6. "I'm just so horny."

> "My ex and I are now friends with benefits. He's familiar to me and when I'm lonely I can just call him up."

> "My ex-girlfriend and I had a terrible relationship but always had terrific makeup sex. We now have terrific breakup sex about once a week."

I've heard dozens of stories from people who think that continuing a physical relationship with their exes is perfectly reasonable. After a breakup, emotions run high, and days can seem long and difficult. Your sensitivities are heightened, and when you see your ex every part of you sits up and takes notice. The air is charged when newly broken-up lovers meet, and you might mistake this for physical connection or arousal. You might have been feeling undesirable or just lonely, and start to think, "Oh, what the hell. What harm could it do?" After all, you know each other; you know what sex is like with each other. What's one more go-round?

While breakup sex seems like fun, it comes with confusion and more complications and is another thing to avoid. Even if you have a terrific time, you will end up feeling confused and maybe even used. Afterwards, you might start to think that your ex has been with someone else, leaving you feeling insecure and emotional. Which means that the drama could start all over again. Even if none of that happens, at the very least you have postponed the inevitable, but it's that time once again: You've got to say goodbye.

Sometimes people try to carry on "just" a physical relationship after a breakup without any of the irksome characteristics of their relationship. They justify it by telling themselves and each other that it's easier this way. They tell themselves that being "friends with benefits" instead of two people in a committed relationship works for everyone. It doesn't.

Continuing a physical relationship after giving up the committed relationship and its inherent responsibilities is a prescription for trouble. Do not buy into "friends with benefits" scenarios.

Benefits must have corresponding responsibilities, and if they don't, you're using each other. So stop it and grow up. There is no such thing as "friends with benefits." There is only "friends who have no idea what they're doing to the detriment of themselves and each other." Don't do it with your ex—or anyone else for that matter. Conduct your life with dignity, and don't give away anything unless the person you're giving it to takes some responsibility toward you, especially if he or she is an ex-lover.

If it's dead, bury it. Don't sleep with it.

7. "We run in the same circles."

"I am a jazz musician in New Orleans. Every musician in this town knows everyone else. I run into my ex all the time and it can't be avoided."

"My ex and I are trying to make a joint-custody arrangement work, so we have to see each other all the time. He's always telling me about these great parties he goes to or these women he's seeing. It drives me crazy."

"I'm a gay man in Dallas. Everyone in this community knows each other, tends to live in the same neighborhood, shop in the same stores, and eat in the same restaurants. I see my ex all the time and I hear about things he's saying about me."

"We work in the same building and often have to go to the same meetings. I see my ex all the time and have overheard her talking about her new boyfriend."

"My ex and I are both Broadway actors. We see each other all the time and are often up for the same parts. I've tried to stop contact but it's impossible when we keep running into each other."

"My ex and I go to the same twelve-step meetings, and she won't give up her meetings and I won't give up mine. I hear about things she's said about the relationship and it's just wrong. I find myself sharing to rebut some of the things she's said and not really saying what I want to be sharing about."

There are many situations where full NC is impossible. Sharing joint custody, being in the same job, working in certain industries, or being a member of certain communities brings us face-to-face with ex-partners we'd just as soon avoid. But even if you work in the same building or department, share custody, or belong to a small, tight-knit community, you can be NC.

In this case, NC means that you don't speak unless it's necessary—and you don't use "bumping into each other" as an excuse to call, e-mail, or text later on. If you are colleagues or co-parents, naturally you have to speak. But keep your conversations brief and to the point, and only talk about the job or the children.

Sometimes people who go to the same support groups or twelve-step meetings need to come to an understanding about how post-breakup meetings will be handled and what each person is going to share at the meetings. Being able to talk about your relationship in a twelve-step meeting is important, but one word of caution: It's also easy to "triangulate" your friends. A message or comment could get carried back to your ex unbeknownst to you. This is not good, not healthy, and not what you go to twelve-step meetings for. You might need to find some women-only or men-only meetings. If you were a gay couple, you might need to agree on certain meetings that will be just yours or just your ex's. Twelve-step breakups can be awkward and painful, so be sure to draw boundaries. You might want to agree to not talk about the relationship in meetings, and keep it between you and your sponsor. Call on your sponsor and close friends, and try to talk to others who have gone through it before and work out a plan. Otherwise it's going to get messy.

Work breakups are similarly difficult. It's hard to be a professional when everyone knows your business. You might need to draw some lines with your ex and agree on saying nothing at work about the breakup. The last thing you need at the office every day is all of your coworkers gossiping about you. Try to talk to your ex about the ground rules for discussing the relationship at work before the rumor mill gets going. Agree to keep it very businesslike, and only share your personal pain with close friends who do not work with your ex. Keep the boundaries very clear.

The same rules apply if you live in a small, tight-knit community. Keep it businesslike, and don't use your community of friends and neighbors as an outlet for getting back at each other or communicating indirectly with each other. Try not to flaunt new relationships, and if your ex does, ignore it. Playing into it in the short term might feel good and may give you the opportunity to let off some steam, but you'll suffer in the long term for it.

Of course, there are situations where you have to see your ex. These will be difficult, but the same rules apply. No random e-mailing or texting, no phone calls. No getting into it about the former relationship or the breakup, no sharing personal information or flaunting new relationships, no jealous rages or manipulations. Keep your side of the street clean even if your ex doesn't. If you must see each other, keep it businesslike and dignified.

Steps to Successful "No Contact"

Sitting with swirling feelings and the compulsion to make contact is very hard to do. It's like breaking an addiction—difficult and sometimes downright painful. So do what you would do if you were trying to kick a habit. Recognize that it's not going to be easy at first, but commit to the process because you will be a better person for it.

The first thing you must do to be successful at NC is affirmatively decide you are not going to contact your ex no matter what. You must make a contract with yourself to stop doing it, which means that you must sit with the uncomfortable emotions until they pass.

You must decide that you will not call, instant message, or e-mail your ex. You also will not check his or her Facebook or MySpace page. This contract with yourself means that you will not put yourself in places where you could have an "accidental" meeting with your ex. You will decide that even if you think you have every reason in the world to connect, you will think it through and not act on it immediately.

Have a support system of people firmly in place so that you can contact them when you feel like communicating with your ex. If you are keeping your emotions bottled up inside, it will be tempting to talk to your ex, so make sure you have a frontline group that you can go to when the temptation gets great. This way you can call people who will support you instead of doing something you will regret later. Make a list of friends and family who are available at different times during the day. You can join both online support groups, such as the GPYP blog and e-mail group, and face-to-face support groups. Gather the troops and let them know when you're having a bad day.

It's hard to stay mentally focused if you're physically run-down. Make sure you are taking enough breaks, getting enough rest, eating right, having fun, and doing nice things for yourself, because if you're not, you will be more tempted to act out. If you haven't been taking care of yourself, start now. See Chapter 4 for more ways to take care of yourself.

Maybe as you have been reading this you have been contacting your ex. If so, start NC now and forgive yourself for the communications you've had. Don't dwell on the mistakes you've made, just resolve to not make them anymore. If you don't start fresh, the guilt and shame you feel over your past behaviors will keep you stuck. One woman told me:

> After we broke up, I stayed in touch any way I could. I called him, I texted him, I e-mailed him. I even went back and spent the weekend with him and was miserable by Sunday night. Now, the biggest challenge for me is feeling guilty and ashamed of myself for acting in such an undignified manner—being needy and seemingly pathetic—for so long. I finally put the "no contact" rule in place, and I can tell you that it is the rule to follow. Since I forgave myself for my slipups, being NC has been liberating.

It is important that you don't dwell on your past mistakes. Put them aside and start "no contact" now.

Exercises to Help You Stay "No Contact"

In behavioral therapy, therapists often ask their clients to keep detailed daily records of particular events or psychological reactions. If you are trying to stop a behavior—compulsive overeating, for example—it helps to keep a food journal detailing not only what you eat but what you are feeling and what is going on in your physical world when you find yourself in trigger situations. By looking at the patterns that emerge in the journal, a client can break the chain before heading to the kitchen to relieve uncomfortable feelings. This journal approach sheds insight on many destructive patterns and habits, and has proven to be a successful tool in combating undesirable behaviors.

Use your journal to log how many times you are communicating with your ex. Write about your reactions when your ex contacts you and your reactions when you make the contact. Write about what is going on for you right before the urge to call comes up. Ask questions before, during, and after. Spend some time with these questions, thinking about them and writing out the answers. You'll have your own questions, but here are some that might help you figure out what is going on:

How was this desire to call triggered?

What are you feeling? Are you anxious, bored, sad, empty, or lonely?

Is there a specific thing (thought, memory, question) driving your desire to connect?

What outcome do you expect?

Where are your expectations coming from? Are they fantasies of what you want to have happen? Or are they based upon what has happened in the past? Are you operating from fantasy or reality?

Are you trying to change the past?

Are you trying to get a certain reaction?

Are you trying to relieve the pain and the pressure?

Do you think negative attention is better than no attention at all?

Do you feel forgotten? Unimportant? Is contact your way to let the person know you still exist?

Are you thinking you can control your ex's moving-on process?

Are you hoping your ex can't really move on as long as you are buzzing around in the background?

What is your motive?

Why are you so focused on this one person?

Wanting to call is like a compulsion, obsession, or addiction, and stopping works the same way. If you are an alcoholic or nicotine addict, you're not going talk yourself into thinking that one day you'll just wake up and not want a drink or a cigarette. Of course not. You will stop the behavior (drinking or smoking) and then all the discomfort will rise up in you. You'll be faced with either dealing with it or going back to practicing your addiction. The longer you practice it, the harder it's going to be to stop.

After journaling you will realize that you need to put some things in place to stop the contact. The next step is to be proactive by planning specific actions that you'll take to resist the urge to make contact. Then make a list of steps to take before you initiate contact or return a call or e-mail.

Here's an example.

STEP ONE: Write in my journal.

STEP TWO: Call a friend or write to an online support group.

STEP THREE: Take a shower.

STEP FOUR: Work with my crafts or hobby.

STEP FIVE: Go for a walk.

STEP SIX: Go to the gym.

As you are doing your predetermined steps, say your affirmations (see page 79) and give yourself positive feedback. Put a plan in place so that you have prescribed steps to take before you call. This allows you to take control and not be blown about by your impulses. It will serve as a guide that tells you what to do when you are in the throes of emotion and having trouble curbing your compulsions.

You may need to experiment with different actions and behaviors and then evaluate which ones work best for you. Take time to think about it. Maybe you need to go somewhere where there are no telephones or computers. Leave your cell phone at home and drive to a park or mall or somewhere where you cannot communicate. Maybe you need to take a nap or watch television. You can invite a friend to the movies, take up a sport, or work out. Perhaps your style is to meditate and visualize your life free of this person and these urges to connect.

It is very important to think about and learn alternative behaviors when you are desperate for contact. Make lists of things you can do, consult your step plan, and have a few alternative step plans. There are many, many things you can do instead of calling.

If all of this is not working, ask yourself: Are you not done yet? Do you need to beat your head against the wall some more? The longer you roll around in the mud with your ex, the longer it will take you to get where you are going—to a new and happy life that you deserve.

The key to getting stronger and moving on is to separate yourself from the relationship and the person with whom you spent so much time. As long as this person is distracting you from your work, it will be difficult to put a period at the end of the sentence that is this relationship and turn to a new chapter in your life. Continuing to seek contact or respond to contact just keeps you stuck and adds to your hurt. It's counterproductive to building a new and meaningful life.

Does it hurt when you do that?

Don't do that.

3

Grief as the Healing Feeling

> Grief will happen either as an open healing wound or as a closed festering wound, either honestly or dishonestly, either appropriately or inappropriately.
>
> ELISABETH KUBLER-ROSS

> Grief is itself a medicine.
>
> WILLIAM COWPER

Time does not heal all wounds. If it did, there would be no unresolved grief and no hurt from long ago that still upsets you from time to time. Pain that is not faced does not go away, it stays inside and festers. If each time you have a loss you deny it, you will end up with a pile of unresolved grief, making each loss harder and harder to cope with.

When people are afraid of being hurt, often because they have not dealt with their unresolved grief, their life becomes narrower, their fear becomes greater, and choices become more difficult to make. With unresolved grief running the show, it is difficult to get close to people and hard to trust anyone.

Fear produces a fight-or-flight response. When it comes to relationships, the flight response manifests itself differently for each person. Some have intimacy difficulties. Some try to get close, feel suffocated, and then run away. Others respond to the fear with the fight response where, after the initial honeymoon period, they disintegrate into endless arguing or a pattern of breakups and make-ups. Most relationship dysfunction can be directly attributed to unresolved loss in one or both partners. Resolving the loss means you will no longer be afraid, enabling you to have happier and healthier relationships.

One of the reasons I became a grief therapist was that my own grief work healed me. I had been an emotional cripple all of my life. I was afraid of being hurt and afraid of being close—all because of my unresolved loss.

Thinking back on the losses was akin to putting my hand on a hot stove. I would recoil every single time. But when the pile got to be too big, I had to give in and work through it. I had to look at all of my losses, feel them, heal them, and then move on. Each time I did that, I became a more confident person, a more alive person. I started to heal and experience true happiness for the first time. I became a grief therapist to help others heal their broken places and experience the joy that is life once you heal your unresolved loss.

Almost every client I have ever worked with resisted acknowledging his or her grief and working through the loss after a breakup. At first the process seems very difficult, because you have to face your true feelings head on. For a time it seems easier to ignore it, but when you ignore loss after loss, it takes an emotional toll that exacts a very high price.

On the other hand, all good things flow from healing unresolved loss. If you have had other unresolved losses, they may have led to a series of difficult relationships. Now you have the opportunity to break the pattern, to heal everything in you that needs to be healed and to learn the lessons you need to learn. Use this time to mend so that you may open one day to lasting love. Once you know how to cope with loss, you will realize that loss is not the end of the world—you can get through it. And once you've worked through a significant loss, you will come out on the other side unafraid, open to new situations and new relationships, able to love fully and give freely. When you are not afraid of grief, you will make better choices. And when you make better choices, you will have happier relationships with healthier people.

Facing your feelings and working through them will give you new confidence and poise. Do the work and resist the urge to fill the void with other things. If you do your grief work while affirming yourself, becoming positive about your life, and developing goals, you will emerge from this experience a better, stronger, richer person. This is the work that will heal you and change your life.

What Is Grief?

Grief is misunderstood by many. I wrote a post on the GPYP blog called "The Emotions of Grief After a Breakup." When I wrote it I hoped that readers would not feel insulted because I had penned something obvious. But the result was exactly the opposite. The post is consistently one of the most popular, and I've gotten dozens of comments expressing relief and gratitude for a post that explains to readers that what they are experiencing is normal. Just knowing that what you are going through is normal and natural, and that there is an end to it, helps in its resolution.

The first thing to know is that grief is not a straight line. It doesn't happen in "stages," as is commonly thought; it happens in phases. The first phase is shock or disbelief; the middle phase is one of review, relinquishment, and great emotion; and the final phase is reorganization, integration, and acceptance.

The phases are not neatly packaged but are rather fluid. People tend to go back and forth between them. This is especially true in the middle phase, where the bulk of the emotional work happens. Because people have been taught to think of grief as happening in "stages," they are often surprised and dismayed to find themselves revisiting a "stage" they thought they had gotten through. Grief is more of a back-and-forth cycling through the phases several times until you finally move, unequivocally, to detachment and acceptance.

Phase One: Shock and Disbelief

> "I could not believe it was over. It was only a few days ago he was talking about getting married. Then he was walking out. It felt like a bad dream and I was sure I'd wake up from it."

> "My wife and I always agreed to couples counseling if there was a problem we couldn't solve. Then she said it was over. I asked if we could see a counselor and she said no; she was moving out

and refused to discuss it further. I had no idea anything was wrong. It hit me like a ton of bricks. I just sat in a chair and stared at the wall for hours. I was shocked. I was numb. I couldn't feel anything."

"We had our issues and one of us was always breaking up with the other. When she left for good it took me a while to realize she wasn't coming back. But even months later a part of me still believed she was and we could put it back together. It took so long for me to deal with it being over for good."

At first you may feel shock or disbelief that a loss has occurred or an inability to recognize that it was really a loss. You know you're hurt, but you want to repress it, suppress it, ignore it, or deny it. Some people can do just that, but it's healthier to recognize that you've sustained a loss. Keep in mind that even if you know it was for the best, you've still had a loss. What have you lost? At the very least you've lost the time, energy, and emotion you put into the relationship. You've also lost the hopes and dreams that you had in the beginning. You've lost the identity of the couple, and you may have lost mutual friends or family members of your ex's that you liked.

Sometimes when a breakup is sudden, the mind goes numb. It shuts down and refuses to face the reality of it for a time. It could be a minute, an hour, a day, weeks, or months. Shock is a protective mechanism designed to keep you from feeling an overwhelming array of emotions. It usually wears off by itself, but sometimes it's worth acknowledging the pain in order to move out of the shock phase.

If you're the one who was left, acknowledge how hurt and rejected you feel. You may feel humiliated and embarrassed, and you may vacillate between acknowledging your feelings and returning to the numbing shock. You may try to start dealing with it, but when you feel the hurt, you quickly shut it down. You might talk yourself into thinking that it's only temporary, and he or she will be back. If you're playing these tricks with yourself, try to acknowledge that chances are good that the relationship isn't coming back, and perhaps it's time to move on from the fantasy that it might. Acknowledge that it's not coming back. Not now. Maybe not ever.

Phase Two: Review, Relinquishment, and Much Emotion

> "I was such a mess that I thought I needed to be hospitalized. I could barely deal with the enormous grief attached to losing someone who had not treated me very well. Going through it was sheer hell."

> "At first I refused to cry, refused to feel badly over it. I wanted to walk away and put my life back in order. But the more I fought the feelings, the stronger they became. Finally I just had to give in. When the feelings first came, I felt like I was going crazy, like my world was upside down. Eventually the pain subsided, but when I was in it, it was not fun."

> "I wanted to kill someone one minute and was a hysterical mess the next. My emotions ran hot and cold. I could be fine and then fly into a rage over nothing. I could be so angry and then

just start crying and wanting to crawl under the blankets. Then I had days where I cared about nothing. I never knew what I'd be feeling next."

If you're the one who didn't see the breakup coming, the shock stage will probably last a while. You feel as if you were punched in the solar plexus or that the world is moving beneath your feet. You may feel an unimaginable void in your world that makes you feel lost and alone, unable to cope. You want to run and hide, but eventually the shock goes away and you are left with the big emotions of grief.

Devastation. Let's go back to the breakup scene. The person you are in love with, and whom you thought was in love with you, says it's over. Even if it was expected, even if you were not getting along, even if you knew there was a chance that things were not going to work out, you are devastated. If you didn't see it coming, you're even more devastated. If it ended because your partner cheated or lied or abused you in some way, it's even more devastating. Even if none of those traumatic things happened, you are still devastated by a powerful sense of loss.

If you've separated from someone who was part of your life, that person's absence will cause you emotional pain. Even if you understand that, you may be unprepared for the searing pain you start to experience. It may upend you, making it difficult to understand where all this pain is coming from. You may feel worse than you ever thought you would or could.

The pain of heartache often comes in unpredictable episodes of intense pain that come and go. These episodes are called grief "spasms"—you feel overwhelmed by your sense of sorrow. You may hurt physically and feel like you have the flu. Consumed by your own pain and situation,you feel disconnected to everyone else and life takes on a surreal, hazy quality. Stumbling through each day, you feel taxed by the most mundane tasks. All you can think about is how much you hurt.

The intensity of your feelings may frighten you, but this is normal. You're not losing control; you're not going crazy. You are grieving.

There will be very difficult periods, but the pain does not last forever. For now, take it an hour at a time, or a minute at a time, or a second at a time—however small the increments need to be for you to get through it. Just know that it doesn't last and you will not always feel this way. Follow the advice in Chapter 4 to take care of yourself, and be gentle with yourself during this difficult time. Reassure yourself that you can and will get through this.

Endless Rumination about Your Ex and the Relationship. Thinking about your relationship in excruciating detail is an important part of the grief process, but it's also the one that can make you crazy. To let go of the relationship, you have to see it for what it is. Your mind switches into overdrive, endlessly processing through the life of the relationship. You can't stop thinking about your relationship or your ex. You recount the breakup scene over and over again, or you relive the happy times. Your mind may bounce back and forth between the breakup and the good times. Your mind thinks about the person you fell in love with and then switches to the person who hurt you. The scenes and conversations flash through your mind randomly, with your emotions reacting to whatever is playing on the movie screen in your brain. The only thing you want to do is shut it off, but you can't.

This constant rumination can be maddening, but, surprisingly, it's psychologically necessary so that you can work through it and be over it. It's not going to last forever, and it doesn't mean you're not going to get over it; it means that you are in the process of getting over it. While it can be crazy-making and seemingly contrary, the constant rumination is about letting go, not holding on.

During this time it's tempting to push the thoughts away and "get busy" with something else. The picture show in your mind is, after all, driving you up the wall! It is helpful to journal about it, talk about it, walk the floors and wring your hands, and curse the process, but let it happen. When you start the Relationship Inventory (page 134), working on it will relieve the images and give you control over the situation. You will still have random thoughts and feelings, but it serves as a good outlet until they subside. Doing the Relationship Inventory harnesses the review and allows you to be the director of the movie.

Disorganization and Confusion. After a breakup, you may also feel physically and mentally incapacitated in some way. You have trouble sleeping, or you sleep too much. You become accident-prone. You have trouble putting a sentence together. You feel scattered and overwhelmed by feelings. You may doubt your ability to function, and maybe your sanity. The emotions seem so big and so unmanageable that you may be afraid that expressing your feelings will result in complete loss of function.

This is normal. Grieving causes confusion and disorganization, as well as disturbance in appetite and sleep patterns. It may disrupt even the most benign daily activities. Grief continually calls attention to itself, and being in disarray is one of those attention-getting devices. It is also a result of your mind's attempt to reorder the world, because the one it knew, the one it was structured around, is now gone.

Confusion and disorganization feel extreme to some people who are experiencing it for the first time. It's hard, but give yourself permission to fall apart; allow yourself the disorganization and confusion. Recognize that you are accident-prone, and take care, especially when driving. Just as people shouldn't drive drunk, they also shouldn't drive when they are in the throes of grief. Recognize when you're not capable of driving, and be responsible toward yourself and others on the road.

Writing in your journal will help you organize your thoughts, but it's also essential to get into the habit of making lists and keeping a calendar. If you've never been terribly organized before, it's going to get worse, so now is the time to write things down and understand that your memory is not in proper working order.

You may be the type of person who has excellent recall. Normally you can think of something you need to do later and when the time comes you remember to do it. That ability will be severely challenged right now. If you pride yourself on an elephant-like memory, you may be surprised to find that the elephant has left the building. Now is not the time for pride, because not putting proper safeguards in place will lead to disaster. Use all the reminders and helpers available to you. Force yourself to write things down, and don't be afraid to ask others for reminders.

Your memory will come back. In the meantime, do what you can to stay on top of things because if you start to fall behind you'll only add to your anxiety, and you don't need this now. Stay as organized as you can, but when you forget things try to be gentle with yourself. It will pass.

Anger. After a breakup, anger is an appropriate reaction. When something has been taken away, people feel angry. While feeling the anger is okay, acting on the anger is not. You can and should acknowledge your anger, own your anger, write about your anger, and talk about your anger. Eventually it will dissipate. What you should not do is act out or lash out in anger. That is not okay.

If you try to repress your anger because you think that it is "unacceptable" or "bad" or "wrong," it will manifest itself in other ways. Some people refuse to acknowledge anger, so they go through life taking it out on other people, irritated all the time, prone to bad moods, and generally being foul and bitter. These are all variations of unexpressed anger. If you have been going through life in an unexplained sour mood, you may have anger issues.

Facing the anger for the first time may result in your feeling not just angry, but rageful. It's good to acknowledge it and let it out, but not to take it out on anyone. Be mindful of your anger when you are driving or interacting with other people so that you don't take your anger out on anyone inappropriately.

Your anger belongs to you.

Own it.

Deal with it.

Here are some ways to help you manage your anger:

Write to the people you are angry with, including your parents and former lovers; just make sure you don't send the letters.

Talk to friends.

Talk to your therapist.

Take a long walk.

Hit a heavy bag.

Smash old dishes.

Exercise.

Scream in the car.

Beat some pillows with a stick.

Rip up paper. (Old cards and letters from your ex are the best.)

Take the opposite tack and try to calm down. Meditate, relax, take deep breaths, and count to ten.

If your anger really feels out of control, see a therapist or a doctor, or enroll in anger-management classes.

Sadness and anger are actually two sides of the same coin. Some say that depression is anger turned inward. Conversely, anger is often sadness turned outward. If you have had trouble connecting with your sadness in the grieving process, you will probably find that expressing anger will lead you to sadness. I once participated in an anger workshop that involved the use of a bat and a heavy bag. Many people had been angry for a long time but were afraid to express it, thinking it would lead to homicidal rage. After being coaxed to express their anger in a healthy way, the opposite happened—the majority broke down in tears as they connected to the sadness buried beneath the anger. Anger work is exhausting, but expressing anger in a healthy way, acknowledging it, and then releasing it is very healing.

Guilt. Guilt is a normal part of the grief process. No matter how well behaved you were in the relationship, you are human, and there will always be guilt about what was done or not done, what was said or not said. There will always be things you wish you could change, but guilt is an unproductive and often counterproductive emotion. Guilt can lead you to think that you caused the breakup and that if you just apologize enough or do things differently, it will all be okay. Getting swept up in guilt is one of the biggest obstacles to moving on, because you can't move on if you still think you can fix it, or obsess about what you did or did not do. Guilt stems from the inability to accept what has happened and a misguided sense that you have power over the situation and can go back and fix it.

But you can't. And even if you could, it wouldn't change the outcome. What happened has happened. Going back is not going to be productive. If you need to write a letter of apology—which you do not send—then do it. But recognize that if you did things wrong that caused this breakup, you need to come to terms with it, accept it, learn from it, and then move on.

Everyone makes mistakes. Even if you made a really horrible mistake, doing this work, healing yourself, and taking responsibility for your actions is the most important form of amends that you can make. Maybe you were the "good guy" but you still feel guilty about perceived shortcomings. If so, go to your journal and write about all the things that you did wrong that are making you feel guilty. Save the list for your Relationship Inventory and Life Inventory, and put the counterproductive guilty feelings away for now.

Anxiety. When going through loss reactions, most people expect to feel sad, angry, upset, maybe even confused. What they usually don't expect to feel is anxious. Sometimes the first wave of anxiety feels like simple restlessness, the need to do something. It may grow worse and become physical: You'll feel agitated and extremely sensitive to noises or movement. You may feel as if your heart is about to leap out of your chest, or perhaps your hands won't stop shaking. The anxiety may interfere with sleeping and eating. The anxiety associated with grief can often feel debilitating and can become chronic. If you are experiencing severe physiological symptoms of anxiety like these, you may want to see your doctor about medication for short-term relief of symptoms.

If the anxiety is not severe enough to warrant medical intervention, try some self-soothing techniques. Set up an atmosphere of relaxation in a favorite room or in your bedroom. Light some candles or use subdued lighting. Put on some soft music and try to relax. Lie down and close your eyes and try to visualize yourself someplace calm like the beach or near a waterfall. If you have trouble with visualization or relaxing on your own, you can buy relaxation, meditation, or self-hypnosis audio recordings. You might want to schedule a massage or some other treatment at a spa. Writing and talking to friends may also help.

Sometimes people struggling with anxiety are also struggling with obsessive thinking, which I will discuss in Chapter 4. If this is an issue for you, you may find relief from anxiety by doing some crafting or coloring. Listen to soothing music and light some candles as you work with your crafts. Try different ways to calm yourself, and understand that the anxiety is another phase that passes fairly quickly.

Ambivalence. Inherent in all grief, including the death of a loved one, is great ambivalence. People usually expect to feel only love and sadness or hate and anger, but are surprised to find that sometimes they feel all of these things—and other times they are not sure how they feel. The grief process can be very confusing, especially when seemingly unrelated feelings rush in and threaten to overwhelm you. Your feelings seem to be going crazy and you can't control them. Other times you're not sure what you feel or if you feel anything at all. Sometimes you feel intense love and then intense hatred, or you may feel deep sadness and then anger. Sometimes emotions turn on and off without warning. Your head tries to sort it all out but cannot get a handle on what you are feeling from one minute to the next. Know that it's okay to not know how you really feel.

Don't try to force feelings if you're not feeling anything or feeling strangely detached. Be thankful for the reprieve. Don't beat yourself up for not feeling how you "should" feel or how others say you should feel. Accept the ambivalence and know that it will probably give way to other feelings when you're ready to process them. Feelings are not right or wrong, they just are. Allow yourself yours.

Pining and Searching. After any loss, the mind tries to put the world back to the way it was. If someone or something is lost, there is an impulse to look for that person or thing. It is the mind's way of reordering the world to the way it "should" be. This results in pining for someone lost and the urge to search.

Pining and searching usually happen when the emotions of grief are at their peak, and it can feel very distressing. Attachment to something familiar makes us feel safe and secure in the world even if the attachment is unhealthy or destructive. When someone or something is taken from us, our first instinct is to look for it to get it back. We want it back the most when we feel the weakest.

Often people who have experienced the death of a loved one experience the urge to search. They will look for a deceased person in a crowd or find themselves dialing that person's phone number. This is a normal and natural part of the grief process whereby the mind tries to suspend reality and restore things to how they were earlier. In a breakup, when the urge to search comes along, this is often when people try to open up communication. But now, when you are pining and searching, you are very vulnerable, so take care to avoid saying anything you will regret later. And remember—this is a temporary state of mind.

This phase is extremely uncomfortable to get through. People who have experienced the death of a loved one find themselves calling that person on the phone or going by his or her house. This is an intensely emotional phase. Obviously, when the person is alive, as after a breakup, you're able to make contact, but you shouldn't, because nothing good will come of it. The pining-and-searching phase is a low point in the grief process, and you don't want to present your most vulnerable state to your ex. Also, there is the danger that the searching can turn into stalking. Not good and not legal. Don't do it. While the urge to search is normal, the actual searching should not be done. Understand that the urge to search is a frustrating and uncomfortable component of grief that lessens with time.

The less you give in to this urge, the easier it gets. You don't want to lose your way, you want to stay strong and know where you are. Tolerate the searching feelings without reaching back.

To get through the urge to search, use the same techniques you use for NC. If you feel agitated because you can't search, try the techniques I suggested for anxiety, because restlessness in searching is similar to it. Write in your journal. Write letters to your ex that you won't mail. Call a friend and ask if you can talk. Go to a movie. Meditate. Relax. Find crafts to do. The urge to search will pass.

Depression and the Need for Clinical Intervention. Breakups are inherently painful. Your hurt is not necessarily a measure of your love for the other person but rather a measure of your humanity. We are humans. We love and we become attached; when we lose a love and need to detach, we hurt. If we've had a number of hurts in the past that we haven't dealt with, we may be prone to depression.

Pain after a breakup, even searing pain and abject misery, is normal and natural. Other normal and natural side effects of grief are pacing the floor, not being able to sleep, anxiety attacks, difficulty concentrating, and a general feeling of malaise. These reactions, even when severe and somewhat debilitating for a day or two, are normal and natural.

Suicidal thoughts or deep depression are not normal. If you are having these reactions, see a professional before doing anything else. Even if you are not suicidal, if you are feeling intense despair or no hope at all, these are signs of clinical depression. You cannot do the work if you cannot function. Grief work impacts daily activities and will make you feel less energetic. You may need to take one or two mental-health days for yourself. But this is not the same as clinical depression. If you are having trouble functioning for more than a day or two, get an evaluation. You could be clinically depressed and need medical intervention.

If at any time in the process you feel so depressed that you cannot function or feel suicidal, see a professional immediately. You don't have to wait to get an appointment. All emergency rooms are equipped to handle these kinds of emergencies, so go to one if you need to. Everyone going through a breakup can benefit from seeing a counselor or therapist, but if you have plunged into a deep depression or have suicidal thoughts, get help immediately.

It is a sign of strength, not weakness, to get help when you need it. It is okay to ask for help, especially when you are in emotional pain. You may need some counseling and/or medication to get through the roughest time. It's okay to need support. It means you're working hard and healing. Don't suffer in silence. Get the help you need.

Other Tips for Dealing with the Middle Phase of Grief

In addition to the earlier suggestions, make sure you take care of yourself during this time by eating right, exercising, and getting enough sleep. Follow all of the self-care suggestions in Chapter 4. Remember to write a positive note in your journal every night. Make sure this note gives you credit for your feelings, for doing the work and getting through that day. After all, it's one less day in the grief process. End every single day on a positive note and know that you are one step closer to being healed. Know that you will have good days and bad days. Sometimes you won't feel like getting out of bed. Other days you will be strangely detached from everything and everyone.

You may start to feel better and life may seem to be going well. You've had glimpses of acceptance and integration and then all of a sudden you're in the emotional maelstrom of Phase Two again. This is called recycling and is very normal. It will be shorter and less intense each time.

Phase Three: Reorganization, Integration, and Acceptance

> "One day I realized it had been a few days since I cried. Then I realized it had been a few days since I thought about him. It came on quietly. I was healing."

> "I thought I had turned a corner, and then I was feeling low again. I kept recycling and thought, 'I am never going to get over it.' I went through a few recyclings before I was out of the emotional woods, but the day came when I could say, honestly, I was over it."

The final phase of grief is acceptance, sometimes referred to as integration or reorganization. Being in this phase doesn't necessarily mean you are happy; it means you are starting to move on and find some peace about the breakup.

Accepting the loss does not mean forgetting or never feeling sad again, but it is a turning point signaling that the final phase of grief has begun. Acceptance is about understanding what has happened and that it cannot be changed. After you have lived through the difficult feelings, there is often the first glimpse of acceptance. Although emotions may reemerge and you will experience the middle phase of grief again, the acceptance phase will return eventually. In time, the periods of peacefully accepting the loss last longer than the periods of sorrow.

During the final phase, a new understanding of life and loss results in profound reorganization of a person's life. People who have worked through a significant loss have new priorities, new values, and a different perspective. This is the time when people tend to make major changes: They will change jobs, return to school, move to another state, or become serious about goals in life. Once you start to feel the acceptance, start working on your goals and plans for the next few years, as outlined in Chapter 4. Even if you return to the emotional work, you will have started to outline goals to revisit and refine when you come back to acceptance.

Integrating the loss means finding a new outlook on life, enjoying life again, and living without guilt or pain. During this phase, people often resume taking care of their own needs and feelings that they denied themselves for so long. Often a sense of courage and strength, absent before the loss, emerges. Integration means giving yourself permission to live life and to love again. It allows you to go forward with a new understanding and a new appreciation for yourself.

One final word on the acceptance phase of grief: It's a very quiet thing, and it comes in phases just like everything else. When you do find it, accept it and enjoy it. It might feel strange and be different than you envisioned it. At times you may have intense moments of happiness and at other times just feel empty, as if something is missing. Or, it can be serene and calm. Make peace with the peace. It means your life is working.

Soon you'll be able to turn the page and help others heal. Let people know that working through your loss was painful, it was hard—but the rewards are amazing. Share your stories with others who are just beginning their journeys so that they can take the same journey that has worked for you.

4

Taking Care of Yourself

One of the most important things you can do for yourself is to take your head out of your ex's life and put it back into yours. When a breakup doesn't make a lot of sense, and sometimes even when it does, it is natural to replay the breakup and the events leading up to the breakup in your mind. This is a phase of grief (see page 54). You relive all the conversations to understand, to try to make it make sense. I've had clients, students, and readers ask me the following questions in every way possible:

How can this be?

Why am I hurting over this person?

What can I do to change things?

Why why why? How how how?

Although these thoughts are normal, the danger is that you can lose yourself in obsession. Obsession is typically defined as recurrent, intrusive thoughts. Be aware that obsession is not the same as the review necessary for grief or reviewing your relationship for your self-growth. Instead, it's choosing to ruminate about situations that you can't change. It's turning things over in your mind searching for answers where there are none. It's thinking and rethinking with no useful purpose.

The questions are automatic when you are dumbstruck by a situation. A woman said to me, "My ex always complimented me on my maturity and then left me for a new person who is immature and spoiled. I just don't get it." Another man said, "I thought it was a phase when it first started. I thought that if I left her alone, she would snap out of it. The next thing I knew she leaving me and saying it wasn't me, she just wasn't feeling it. I can't help wondering what I did wrong or what I missed."

Sometimes the person we thought we knew changes before our eyes even in long-term relationships. One woman said, "After four years my boyfriend suddenly became self-absorbed and depressed and pushed me away. The person I knew is gone and I can't comprehend it." A gay man who argued with his family over his lover and then moved to a distant city so they could be together said, "He promised so many things. We got to a new city, and he suddenly dumped me. Despite begging me to move here, he now says he never did, which is completely untrue. I'm not only hurt and alone but I can't make sense out of how this happened." It's hard to stop the questions, but to move on, that is what you need to do.

Sometimes, instead of accepting a reality that doesn't make sense, we tell ourselves: It just can't be this way. Something will change. This is temporary. I'll just sit here and wait for my love to smarten up and see the light. Better yet, I will *change* things.

Eventually the new reality does sink in and with it, the crushing feelings of hurt, anger, betrayal, and rejection. You might begin to wonder how you can turn yourself into, or back into, someone that this person will love. I'll be quieter, thinner, happier. I won't complain so much. I won't rock the boat. I'll like the insufferable family and friends whom I couldn't stand before. I'll go back to school. I'll stop going to school. I'll wear different clothes. I'll buy a new car. I'll get those allergy shots so I can be around that cat. I'll work in a different industry. I'll muzzle my kids. I'll clean more. I'll clean less. I'll cook gourmet meals. I'll listen when spoken to. I'll go to bed earlier. I'll go to bed later. I'll go to church. I'll stop going to church. . . . I'll do it all. I'll do nothing. I'll be more. I'll be less. I'll be everything and anything other than what I'm being right now. I'll turn myself inside out to be the person he or she will love. I can do it. I will do it.

You may immediately think that you need to change yourself in order to change the situation, but that isn't so. Stop worrying about what is wrong with you. While there might be things about you that need improvement, that doesn't mean that you are not a lovable, worthwhile person. In fact, it takes a lovable, worthwhile person to become willing to grow and get better.

You have to decide that you are going to get back in your own head. So long as you are stuck in the why, what, and how questions and worrying about what your ex is or is not doing, you are postponing your own moving on. Certainly, if your ex has done something very out of character or against everything you believed to be true, it is hard to stop rehashing it. Combating this kind of obsession takes decision and discipline. When you are asking why, when, how questions or trying to figure out how he or she could do what was done or how you can change into the person he or she will love, tell yourself, "It doesn't matter, it doesn't matter, it doesn't matter." Yes, three times is the charm with this particular mantra. Whenever you are ruminating and obsessing about your ex and asking those questions, say to yourself, "Stop! It doesn't matter, it doesn't matter, it doesn't matter." Because you know what? It doesn't matter.

The only thing that matters is what you are doing now and that is where your focus needs to be. Whenever you are in someone else's head, no one is taking care of yours! Stop asking questions about your ex; start asking questions about you.

Putting the Focus Back on Yourself

As you are no doubt experiencing, moving on from your past relationship involves feeling and expressing pain, anger, confusion, and frustration. In addition to feeling your feelings, the road to healing includes reviewing your relationship and examining unfinished business from the past. You need to go out and meet new people, do new things, and learn a different way of being. You need to plan for the future while dealing with the present and taking a hard look at your past. All of this is difficult and demanding.

The only way to stay committed to this challenging work is to balance it with positive, life-affirming actions. Not only will this solidify your commitment to the healing process, it will help keep a sense of stability in your life during this potentially unsettling time. Throughout this process, remember that nature abhors a vacuum so balance is key to everything you do. When you are doing your challenging emotional work, you must try to balance it, every day, with being good to yourself, which includes

journaling your thoughts and feelings;
affirming yourself with kind, loving, and positive thoughts;
erasing your negative self-talk;
making gratitude lists;
combating obsessive thoughts;
developing goals;
giving yourself credit and taking frequent breaks from the work;
treating your physical self well;
spending at least one night a week doing nice things for yourself; and
finding support.

This chapter discusses in detail the self-care steps you need to take, so you'll want to keep coming back to it throughout the grieving and healing process.

Journaling: Writing It Out

Although it might seem more like work than "self-care," keeping a journal is one of the most vital parts of the healing process. Think of your journal as a companion through a difficult time where you work out the bad and work in the good. Grief is about letting your feelings out, and success is about positive self-talk and planning. Journaling allows you to do both, and to make sure that the two are in balance. In the aftermath of a bad breakup there are many things to feel, to learn, to think about, to plot out, and to plan for. Your journal keeps it all straight. It not only helps you work out what you're going through emotionally, but also helps you turn your goals and dreams into a concrete plan of action. Through your journal you can see where you've been and where you are going, make adjustments, and figure out your next step.

All permanent change starts with an awareness of how you are and how you want to be. Learning to sit back and observe your thoughts and feelings, as well as the people around you, is a powerful tool that gives you control of your life. Write your observations in your journal even if you are not sure what they mean yet. Eventually these will lead you to the patterns in your life and the unfinished business that needs to be finished.

Prepare to make journaling part of your everyday life by thinking about the kind of journal that will best facilitate your writing. Do you want a notebook, an expensive diary, a special book? Will you journal on the computer? It might help to have a small pad or digital recorder with you throughout the day to record thoughts and later transfer them to your computer in the evening. A seminar student bought a beautiful pen he really liked because he thought it would help him journal and it did. Another woman bought a blank book and decorated the outside, and still another used a loose-leaf binder so she could take a few pieces of paper along with her each day and put them in the binder at night. Whatever you decide, make it personal to you and make it something you will definitely utilize in the weeks ahead.

Cultivate the habit and spend some time each day writing down what's going on for you and the steps you are taking to move beyond loss. How are you feeling? What are you doing? What are you trying to change in your life? After a few weeks, it will become second nature to you and its effect on you will be evident. Throughout this book I instruct "write it in your journal" because writing it out is an important part of moving forward.

Affirmations and Positive Self-Talk

> "Affirmations have made an incredible difference in my life. No matter how much talk therapy I did or how many meetings I attended, I couldn't seem to shore up my low self-esteem. Affirmations did the trick."

> "Working on my positive self-talk has made me a happier person. The difference is subtle at first but then you realize your outlook and attitude have changed and you're seeing the good in things."

> "I don't think I would have progressed as far as I have in as short a time without the affirmations. Learning to write them and saying them every day has changed everything."

Before you can build good and healthy relationships with others, you must have a good and healthy relationship with yourself. No one else can love us more than we love ourselves. A happy and healthy life starts with a positive self-image and high self-esteem. But if your self-esteem is not that high, you can increase it.

There are many reasons your self-esteem may be low right now. Maybe it's been in short supply all of your life or maybe your normally high self-worth has taken a beating during this last relationship and breakup. Ending a relationship can leave you feeling not just lonely, but painfully aware of your shortcomings. Perhaps you've been focusing on what you did or said wrong and have started to think that it's all your fault and that you are a terrible person. Perhaps your ex-partner moved on to someone new and you're comparing yourself to this person. If you had any self-esteem when your relationship ended, it may be dwindling now that your ex is with someone else. If this new person seems to be everything you are not, the self-denigration can become chronic.

Regardless of whether you've lived with low self-worth for a few weeks or all your life, it's time to change it with positive self-talk, affirmations, and visualization. We'll discuss each of these aspects in turn.

Self-Talk

We all give ourselves thousands of messages a day about who we are. As we go through our daily interactions and activities, we record, in our mind's eye, what we are doing, saying, and feeling. Then we engage in self-assessment about our behaviors, and that self-assessment can be brutal. For example, if you forget something, you might say to yourself, "I can't believe I forgot that! I'm so stupid." You may not even be aware that you speak to yourself in this way because it's so ingrained. When I've used this as an example in seminars, people have raised their hands and said, "Well, if I do forget something, I am stupid!" Somewhere along the line these people were told that forgetting something is equal to being stupid.

But it's a message that, no matter how ingrained, is not true. Everyone forgets things and doing so doesn't mean you're stupid.

But when we view normal imperfections and mistakes as character flaws, we can't possibly maintain a positive self-image. And when we don't have a positive self-image, we settle for unhealthy partners and bad relationships. Therefore, this negative self-assessment must stop. But remember, nature abhors a vacuum so it's not enough to just stop it; you must change to positive self-assessment with affirmations.

Affirmations

You may have heard about affirmations (positive declarations), and maybe you doubt that they can work for you. You may have even tried them a time or two without results. If this has been your experience, you're right: Not all affirmations work. There are many bad examples of affirmations available in books, on audio recordings, and on the Internet. But give them another try, because affirmations *done correctly* are very powerful tools.

How do affirmations work? Affirmations feed messages to your subconscious mind about your identity. To understand how this happens, it's helpful to understand how the subconscious works. The subconscious forms your skills, habits, tendencies, and self-image. But although its role in your life is powerful, it works on a very basic level. The subconscious mind is simple and habitual. It is simple in that it

understands only discrete, easy concepts;
takes statements literally;
doesn't know the difference between reality and suggestive thinking;

knows only the present;
does not understand negative phrasing or anything that is not there at the moment; and
responds very well to visualization.

It is habitual in that it

responds to repetition and imprints repetitive messages;
does not "un-imprint" easily; and
can be programmed through repeated suggestions.

These characteristics illuminate why your low self-worth exists in the first place and why affirmations can change it. As a child, you were given messages about who you are by parents, peers, or others, and your subconscious imprinted them. The result is your self-image. If you started out with negative messages from others, you not only have a negative self-image but you may have also gravitated to others who confirmed and reinforced your low opinion of yourself. But it's now the time for you to be in control of the programming and in charge of your life. If you feed your subconscious positive messages in the manner it understands, your subconscious will reprogram all your negative ideas.

Although affirmations have the power to reverse all the negative feedback you've had over the course of your life, your subconscious does not let go of old ideas easily; therefore, the retraining must take place throughout each day. To "unprogram" your mind you must work at planting the seeds, repeatedly and consistently, several times each day. But the good news is that once your subconscious is reprogrammed, it will be hard to deprogram those new ideas. So if you put thought, time, and energy into your affirmations and positive self-talk, you will not only undo a lifetime of negative imprinting, but once your self-esteem goes up, it will stay up. Affirmations are worth the effort because the payoff is tremendous.

There are several ways to affirm. The first is to stop your negative self-talk with what I call "spontaneous interruption affirmations." This is used when you catch yourself speaking badly of yourself, berating yourself, or buying into someone else's criticism of you. Combating these negative thoughts is a combination of thought-stopping and a positive statement. Let's take the earlier example in which you forget something and say, "I can't believe I forgot that! I'm so stupid!" Using the spontaneous interruption technique, you'll say, "Stop! I'm smart!" Thought-stopping followed by a positive statement cuts off the negative self-talk and rewards you with a new view.

The second way is with proactive affirmations, of which there are three types: self-soothing affirmations, image-improvement affirmations, and action affirmations.

1. Self-soothing affirmations assure you of what you already are, reinforce positive things that you already believe about yourself, and work to reassure you when you are anxious or upset. It is helpful to say a few flattering affirmations each day such as "I have nice eyes" or "I am a good worker" or something that you already believe about yourself. It's also helpful to develop some encouraging affirmations to use when you are having a bad day such as "I am okay," "Everything is fine," or "I am getting through this difficult day." Another way to self-soothe is to acknowledge your growth and give yourself credit. You can say, "I am healing" or "I

work hard and enjoy the rewards" or just gently remind yourself to trust the process. Self-soothing affirmations are important because they get you in the habit of caring for yourself through nurturing inner dialogue.

2. Image-improvement affirmations move you toward positive change that you want to effect in yourself. These are changes you want to see in yourself in the days and weeks ahead. They can consist of messages about your overall image ("I am confident") or about a particular part of your image you want to improve ("I get a manicure once a week").

3. Action affirmations move you toward your goals by addressing areas where you need to take steps. These affirmations usually address a goal you want to reach (saving money, returning to school), a habit you want to break (smoking, overeating), or a habit you want to get into (exercising, getting up on time).

Once you begin working with affirmations you will understand how to use them in any given situation, whether it's to soothe you when you feel anxious, to shore up your self-esteem, or to effect a change you want to see in your life.

How to Start Practicing Your Affirmations

Observation: Capture Your Negative Self-Talk

All affirmations begin with observation. Although it's important to stop the negative self-talk as it occurs, you also need to tune into and record, in your journal, the things you say about yourself on a day-to-day basis. Listen—really listen—to your thoughts and comments about yourself and write them down. Then set aside some time to work with them. To start, for each negative thing you say, write in your journal the positive affirming statement. For now, just write the opposite of the negative statement, and we'll talk more specifically about phrasing in a moment. For example, if you catch yourself saying, "I always mess up," change it to "I do things right." Cross out each negative message that you tell yourself and write the positive equivalent instead. Now that you have a good idea of what type of affirmations you need to write, you can prepare your own affirmations around areas you want to work on.

Preparation: How to Write Effective Affirmations

Remember the characteristics of the subconscious as you are writing and saying affirmations. Your subconscious mind is literal, knows only the present moment, does not understand what isn't there, and does not understand vague or abstract concepts. Think of your subconscious as a small child you need to explain things to very definitely and precisely. Small children only know what they see and hear. Concepts such as time, distance, and location (as in "not here") are confusing to them. At the same time, though, you must be brief—after all, children have short attention spans. In sum, effective affirmations must be positive, present, personal, corrective, brief, and concise.

Positive. The subconscious does not recognize what isn't there or what doesn't exist, so effective affirmations are phrased in the positive. This means that you should leave out the word *not* from your affirmations, as well as any contraction that contains *not*, such as *don't*, *won't*, and *can't*. For example, if you're trying to stop smoking and want to write an action affirmation for yourself, your instinct might be to write, "I am not a smoker." But the subconscious has no idea what *not* is, and ignores it. This turns your affirmation into "I am a smoker," which is exactly the opposite of what you want to reinforce! An effective affirmation you could use instead is, "I am smoke-free." If you need extra reinforcement, you can write other action affirmations and include reasons you are smoke-free. For example, you could write, "Because I am healthy, I am smoke-free."

Present. The subconscious only recognizes the present. So avoid phrases like *I want to be . . .* or *I am getting . . .* or *I will be. . . .* Avoid anything that takes you out of today. Other future-sounding phrases to avoid are: *I am going to*, *I will*, and *I should.* You want to tell yourself that you are a certain way, not that you will eventually be that way. Avoid *can* and *could* or *would.* These words suggest that you could be a certain way if you wanted to, but you might not want to. Just because you can be something doesn't mean that you are. The idea is to train the subconscious to think of you in terms of what you are (what you want to be), not what you can be.

Personal and Corrective. Your affirmations should always include a few self-soothing affirmations that reinforce the positive things about you. But overall, your affirmations should move you toward something better—toward something you want or something you want to be.

Your affirmations must serve to help you make the improvements you, personally, need to make. One reason boilerplate affirmations usually don't work is that they mean nothing to you and what needs to change in *your* life. Therefore it's important to make the affirmations your own. Once you've written down your affirmations, review each one to be sure it not only builds a positive self-image, but also means something to you and moves you in the right direction for your life.

One example I use in my seminars is a client who returned to school and was struggling. She had always believed she was smart and capable and was saying self-soothing affirmations that reinforced that, but she was still battling her self-image as a bad student. Just reassuring herself that she was smart and capable did not seem to be working that well. She had been programmed by her family to believe she was not a good student because they had picked apart her study habits and her methods of doing schoolwork when she was younger. Eventually she stopped caring about school and dropped out. Her subconscious was convinced she was not a good student and, therefore, that belief was realized in her waking life.

Going back to school after many years was difficult for her, and she was having trouble in her first semester. So we sat down with her affirmations. The first one she wrote was, "I am a good student." This is a start, but I encouraged her to make the statement personal, to make it her own. What did being a "good student" look like to her? What specific actions could she take that would make her a better student?

She said that as a child she never put enough time into her studies, so she wrote, "I study more." But, again, "more" is vague—too vague to be effective. I asked her to think about what she needed to study and how much she needed to study. Because she was having trouble with her history class and procrastinating on her reading, she wrote: "I am a good student who studies history for one hour every night."

Now her affirmation was concrete. But was it overreaching? If you set your sights too high, you can undermine yourself. I asked her, what about weekends? Are you going to study for an hour seven nights a week? Do you really need to? She thought about it and changed the affirmation to: "I am a good student who studies history for one hour Mondays, Wednesdays, and Thursdays." For her, that worked, and she was able to stick to it while imprinting the affirmation and changing her view of herself.

In this case, what made this student's affirmation corrective was recognizing, realistically, what specific steps she needed to take to change her view of herself as a good student. Once she figured that out, she wrote very effective affirmations to help her study habits. She did well in that class and in all her future classes.

Brief and Concise. The subconscious needs everything spelled out concisely. An affirmation such as "I am getting better every day" is meaningless, not just because of the word *getting* (as we just discussed) but also because of the word *better*. Better at what? The affirmation doesn't say, and therefore it doesn't mean anything to your subconscious mind. If you said to a small child, "I need you to act better," the child would give you a puzzled look. Better than what? Even if you know it means "better than you're acting now," most children under the age of seven will have no idea what you are talking about. And so it is with your subconscious. You need to tell it what you mean by "better." If you want to feel better every day you can say, "I am strong today." But it's even more effective to break it down into what "strong" looks like to you. Think about it and make it as definite as you can: "I am confident." "I am self-assured." "I am graceful." "I am dignified." "I meet challenges as they come." "I overcome adversity." "I rise to the occasion."

Using the techniques we've discussed, here are some examples of taking good affirmations and making them better by making them specific:

Good	Better
I am responsible.	I pay my bills on time.
I am attractive.	I have nice eyes.
I attract good people.	I have loving people in my life. I have positive people in my life. I have kind people in my life. I am treated with care and respect by others.
I am loving.	I treat others with care and respect.
I love myself.	I treat myself with care and respect.
I have a good memory.	I write things down to remember them.
I am prompt.	I write my appointments down in my date book. I arrive at work on time. I arrive at social gatherings on time.
I do my self-care.	I write in my journal every day. I take my vitamins every day. I say my affirmations every day.
I exercise.	I walk to and from work every day. I go to the gym on Mondays, Wednesdays, and Fridays.
I get enough sleep.	I go to bed at 11 p.m. every night.
I am a friendly person.	I say hello to my neighbors.

Cultivation: Keeping Your Practice Going

Although it's important to do spontaneous interruption affirmations whenever you have a negative thought about yourself, cultivating your self-image needs to be more structured. To reprogram old ideas, the subconscious needs consistent imprinting; this is where the proactive affirmations make a big difference. However, if you write too many affirmations you dilute their power because you can't possibly repeat affirmations all day long. So, sit down and write many proactive affirmations and spend time working with them to make them the best they can be. Then pick out seven to twelve proactive affirmations to say several times a day.

Cultivation of your affirmations must happen several times a day, every day. This might mean getting up a bit earlier or setting aside some time at night to read them and really hear what you're saying. Find a few other times a day to read or say them as well. This repetition will really imprint them on your subconscious. Some people choose to write their affirmations on index cards and tape them to the bathroom mirror or put them on their desk at work. Some people record them and listen to them all day long. Whatever works for you, do it!

It takes at least thirty days for a new affirmation to imprint on your subconscious, so use your main seven to twelve for at least thirty days. Then revisit them. Don't change the entire set; just decide whether to refine some, swap some out, or add a few more. Do your affirmations for another thirty days and then revisit them again.

Throughout the days and weeks ahead, affirm that you are capable, confident, and doing well. Make affirmations, positive self-talk, and self-soothing a part of your life. Be your own best cheerleader.

Visualization

While saying your affirmations is an essential part of the process, the home run of imprinting occurs when you take the time to visualize them. Remember, the subconscious responds well to visual stimuli, so this exercise adds an important layer to the process of internalizing your new, positive self-image. Visualization and relaxation speed up the process of change.

Set some time aside each week to do the following steps. First, go somewhere that you'll be comfortable. Sit in a comfortable chair, lie on your bed, or take a bubble bath. Put on a meditation or a relaxation audio recording and close your eyes. Allow yourself to become very relaxed. Think about your affirmations. If you have them prerecorded, play them. If you don't, pick a couple that you can work with and visualize yourself already being in the place you're trying to move toward. Spend time sitting there and really seeing, in your mind's eye, the affirmation coming true.

Another good habit to develop is thinking about them before you fall asleep. Try this at night because it's good to visualize affirmations when the body is relaxed and the tensions of the day are melting away. A student of mine was a businessperson whose colleagues often lectured at symposiums. She wanted to do the same, knowing it would be a boost to her career, but she had a fear of public speaking. She spent a lot of time writing different affirmations that said she was confident and poised and relaxed. She spent several weeks breaking down what a successful public speaker looked like and worked on affirmations around it. Every night as she was falling asleep she would visualize herself giving a talk to a large crowd. At least once a week she spent an hour or so relaxing and visualizing herself speaking in front of an audience. Within six months she gave her first lecture at a major symposium and delightedly reported that she was, in her boss's words, "a tremendous success!" Visualization really works to enforce the affirmations and cement your new self-image firmly in your subconscious.

Visualization is a very powerful tool. You will subconsciously move toward your new self and your new life and the results will be amazing.

Gratitude Lists

The next item of self-care is a short, simple but very powerful exercise: writing gratitude lists.

When you are feeling down, it's easy to lose sight of how much you have in your life. While you do your grief work and allow yourself to feel as bad as you really feel, you must also take time each day to consider the good things you have. This helps foster a positive attitude and is another self-care item that helps you come back into balance as you continue doing the difficult work that can feel so negative. To maintain perspective, write gratitude entries in your journal every day.

When my own therapist first suggested this to me, I was in a bad place. My marriage had recently ended, I had taken my kids and left my house and pets, I had no job, and I was terribly depressed. Not only did everything seem bleak in the present and future, but I had just opened the can of worms that was my painful past. I couldn't imagine times being worse.

So when my therapist told me to write down every positive thing in my life, I couldn't think of a single thing. She told me to write down that I had clothes. I looked at my clothes. They weren't nice and didn't fit. Why would I write about that? She told me to write it down anyway, and I wrote that I had a pair of pants and a closet to hang them in. It seemed silly, but I had no ideas of my own, so I did it.

My assignment was to write gratitude entries every day, once in the morning and once at night. In the beginning my gratitude lists were very basic. Almost every night I wrote that I was grateful for my children. I was grateful for nice weather. I was grateful when I had a hot meal or a hot shower. It was not that I didn't normally have these comforts, but I realized that many people did not. Soon, I started to feel grateful when the car started or when I was in a short line at the grocery store. As time went on, I started going through my days looking for things for my daily entries and noticing many things that actually went right throughout the day.

Several weeks after starting my gratitude work, I felt more positive. Even though I was doing very difficult grief work and looking at my past, life started to get better. I was able to track my success by my growing gratitude lists. Even during my darkest days I could find something to be grateful for, and that made all the difference in the world.

Thinking about what you're grateful for doesn't take away from grieving the end of your relationship, but rather helps keep it balanced. Whenever I finished slogging through writing a letter to my ex in my journal or looking at some painful childhood memory, I would take a break, do something nice for myself, and then come back and write a gratitude list. This helped me work through many a difficult day.

Gratitude lists boost you when you are feeling sorrow and distress because they give you a sense of the good you have in your life and why it's worth it to continue the work. Write these things down and watch those lists grow as you take care of yourself.

Combating Obsessive Thoughts

To stop your obsessive thoughts and ruminations about your ex, you have to replace them with something. A seminar student said she is a very anal-retentive person who likes order and planning. When she became too obsessed with questions about her ex, she would make detailed lists of things she needed to do or buy. Although lists are not for everyone, my student's idea of giving your mind a new focus is right on target. When people complain of either anxiety or obsession, I often suggest that they take up a hobby or learn something new. It can be as major or as minor as you want it to be and it should personally suit you.

Crafts and Hobbies

If there isn't something you've always wanted to do or an interest you've always wanted to pursue, try taking a trip to the local craft store to see if there is something that you would find entertaining or absorbing. Sometimes when people are feeling low, they don't want to be too challenged. It may sound silly, but the act of coloring is very calming. You can color in a book with crayons like you did as a child or fill in intricate patterns with colored pencils. Craft stores sell mandalas, which are intricate designs found in eastern and Native American cultures. Many meditation teachers believe that coloring mandalas allows creativity to flow and leads to an altered state that is healing and insightful. I still have a mandala that I did during a time of debilitating anxiety many years ago. Working with colored pencils and filling in the small spaces helped to steady my hand and calm my mind. I've kept it over the years as a good reminder to refocus whenever I get obsessive about something.

Even if you're not a craft person, you might find something enjoyable like making a dried-flower arrangement or a mosaic candy dish. You might be intrigued by something more elaborate like learning to crochet, woodworking, or stained glass. But go to the store to get some ideas of different things you can do, because working on a project helps you focus your mind while keeping your hands busy, a combination that alleviates both obsession and anxiety. For more relaxation, put on soothing music and light some candles as you work.

If crafts don't do it for you, find something else. Write a book, or learn about photography or astronomy or anything that is fun and interesting. Find a community project to get involved with; buy some language tapes and learn a new language. You might want to learn computer programming, Web design, or animation. These things require concentration and use up a lot of time! A coaching client took up sewing and fashion design, which not only kept her busy but revealed a hidden talent. She is now planning to enroll in fashion-design school. Another client took up garden design, and still another decided to study famous buildings and architects.

Perhaps you've always wanted to collect something. Research the market and study the possibilities of making this happen.

You may come up with something very personal and unique. A seminar student who is a film buff shared with the class that his thought-stopping project was reviewing his top fifty movies of all time. First he decided what they were, then he put them in order, and then he reviewed them. He was nowhere near finished when his obsession ended, but he had fun while doing it.

These exercises are intended to train your brain and let it know that you are in charge. These exercises are not for you to develop an affinity for crafts, learning languages, or studying astronomy. Find something mentally challenging to do—don't just sit around being the victim of your own head. Remember: Nature abhors a vacuum so if you take something OUT you have to put something IN. You can't just stop something, you have to start something else. Take control of your life and decide what that will be.

Rubber-Band Technique

A tried and true behavioral-therapy technique is to put a rubber band on your wrist and snap it every time you think of your ex and what he or she is doing. All that snapping will drive you crazy after a while and you'll stop thinking about it.

Write about It

If you've tried all these thought-stopping techniques but seem to drift back too often to the same old questions, perhaps you need to write a letter that you won't send. Perhaps there's a single question you'd like to ask and it just reverberates in your head over and over again. If so, sit down and write it in your journal. *Do you miss me? Did you ever love me?* Sometimes just the act of writing it down gets it out of your system. You will see that there is no answer, and even if there was one, it would never satisfy you. So go ahead and write a letter you've been wanting to write or ask the question you've been wondering about. Just don't send it.

Combining Techniques

Use some or all of these techniques to train your wandering mind. Again, personalize it and decide what is going to work and how you are going to implement it. A blog reader uses both the rubber-band technique and the technique of changing her ex's name into something useful. She said:

> I've been using the thought-stopping and it helps, so thanks for that. I snap my wrist band and then quickly turn my ex's name in another (healthier) direction. I turn GARY into G (Gratitude for all I have in my life) A (Act as if) R (Reject the rejector and/or keep reaching out) Y (Yes to new experiences, yes to my own life).

Her ex's name, once a source of displeasure, now represents the positive things in her life.

A coaching client said:

> The most instructive thing I learned to stop the thoughts was to continually refocus and reframe back to me. Whenever my mind wandered to him, I would bring it back to me by writing

out the question and then answering it by saying, "It doesn't matter!" I tried the rubber-band technique and the "Stop!" technique. It all works. I know I need to do some looking at my ex, but what he did is not as important as what I allowed. My process is about me and my moving on.

That is precisely what this is all about: your moving on. At some point you need to stop dwelling on what was done to you and start thinking about how you will change things from here on in.

Setting Goals

Keeping your mind busy with new activities is great—for a while. This sort of distraction has an important role in your healing process, but then it's time to retrain your brain to focus on your future.

To become your own person and live your own life, it's important to think about your goals and how to reach them. Deep inside you know who you are, what you want, and what would make you happy. Even if you've suppressed dreams or stopped trying to do certain things, part of you has held on to your dreams and still wants many of these things to come to fruition. Whether it's something big like going back to school or something fun like learning to play the piano or something practical like learning to save money, you have the capacity to know—really know—what would make you happy. Deep down there is an authentic self that yearns for you to take some time to plan and meet those goals.

Goal setting works best when you have long-term goals and short-term goals in different areas of your life. Of course, you're not going to have goals in every area, but you want to choose enough different ones to sustain your interest. Some examples of goal areas are

Family relationships and your home;
Humanist, volunteer, philanthropy, ethical;
Social, cultural, travel, entertainment;
Finances, career, education;
Physical, diet, exercise; and
Fun.

How to Set Goals

Look at the list and spend some time journaling about things you want to achieve in a few different areas. Then pick five to seven goals and decide which one you want to work with first. The key to succeeding with each goal is to make it realistic and then break it down into manageable pieces. Each long-term goal is made up of several short-term goals. For example, if you want to save $1,000 in ten months you need to save $100 a month or $25 a week. So you need to plan a budget that leaves you with $25 per week in savings.

To help with your goal of saving money, develop some affirmations such as "I am good with money" or "Because I am good with money, I save $25 a week." Next, visualize yourself putting $25 a week in the bank and experience the satisfaction of having $1,000 after ten months. No matter what your goal you can break it down into manageable pieces and work through each piece to achieve the long-term goal.

Look at your long-term goal to make sure it's realistic. Don't set your goals too low or too high. If your goal is to save money and you're making $100,000 a year, saving $200 in five years is not difficult. In fact, it's entirely too easy. If you want to lose 100 pounds in six months, it's not doable, it's not healthy, and setting a goal like that is defeating. Don't set impossible goals. That's just going to reaffirm a negative message that you can't do what you set out to do.

Create a goal worksheet that includes clear-cut strategies for your short-term goals. Write down any possible obstacles and set a completion date. Make the worksheet very detailed as to what steps you need to take to reach your long-term goal. For each goal, journal about it, think about it, do your research, and figure out what fits best in your life. Remember, observation, preparation, and cultivation. Be methodical. Don't have so many goals that you're quickly overwhelmed and can't do any of them. Don't have goals that are impossible to reach and very frustrating. Check your progress with your goals once a week or once a month. Give yourself lots of credit and even small rewards for sticking to your goals and making them happen.

As you move past negative self-talk and obsessive thinking, the planning and goal setting should become a bigger part of your daily self-care. As time goes on, spend part of each day planning your future.

Take Frequent Breaks

Another important part of this process is taking charge of your life. Life is not what happens to you, life is what you make happen. One way to start taking charge is to schedule frequent breaks and become disciplined about doing the work. During early grief, it may be too much to think about structuring your time. But after a few weeks, it's time to build some structure into your moving-on process. When you're having an emotional day, it's okay to cry; it's okay to feel terrible for a few hours. But then it's time to take a break and do something nice for yourself. When you start doing some of the difficult work we'll discuss in this book, it might be tempting to try to knock it all out in a few days, but it's easy to get inundated that way.

Frequent breaks will help you achieve the balance you need to truly heal and will help you plot a course for your life. Become a person in charge of your emotions and process instead of letting them control you. If you've been crying for a while, decide that it's time to get up and take a walk. If you've been socializing too much and not journaling, plan a night to go home and write about where you are now. Do not allow your emotions to lead you around and decide what you are going to do. Be the leader and the one who makes the decisions about your own life.

Self-Care: Learning to Treat Yourself Well

"After a breakup, it's easy to just slog through each day, feeling bad. When I started doing nice things for myself and spending time with me and for me, the journey became a little easier."

"My focus after the breakup was that I was rejected goods. I stopped taking care of myself and didn't care about my appearance. After attending a GPYB seminar, where the emphasis is on self-care, my routine changed dramatically and I was on the road to healing. It starts with being good to yourself."

"I grew up in a family where giving yourself attention would be deemed selfish and vain. Learning to put me first was one of the hardest, but best, things I've ever done."

When you are not balancing the hard work of healing with the nurturing of self-care, you stop being interested in doing the work to move forward. The foundation for your difficult work is taking care of yourself in mind, body, and spirit. This is an essential daily task. We've just discussed the mind, so it's time to discuss body and spirit.

Taking Care of Your Physical Self

Your heart feels heavy, your brain is learning a lot of new concepts, and you want nothing more than to relax. Relaxation is highly recommended, but don't let it come at the expense of taking care of your physical self. Do not allow yourself to disintegrate at this time. If your sleep or appetite is very disturbed, see your doctor. Here are some steps you can take on your own to take care of your physical self:

1. Eat right. If you cannot stand the thought of food, try protein drinks or meal-replacement bars. Take vitamins and supplements.

If you are diving into food as a comfort, stop. Avoid sugar, fat, and energy drinks. If the breakup is new and you are feeling raw, you may be having trouble avoiding comfort foods. If this is the case, try to get the healthiest form you can—for example, sugar-free ice cream, oatmeal with sugar substitute and low-fat milk, or a baked potato with strips of chicken and low-fat cheese.

2. Get enough sleep. After a breakup, many people will sleep too much or too little. If you are not sleeping, talk to your doctor. If you are sleeping too much, try to limit your sleep each day.

3. Exercise. After a breakup, people often feel as if they don't have the stamina to exercise. It's easier to crawl into a ball and hope the world goes away. But exercise is good not only for your body but also for your mind. Sustained activity releases endorphins, which are "feel good" hormones. Exercise helps you not only look your best, but also feel your best.

4. Don't drink or take drugs. These will just numb the pain and delay dealing with it. These temporary panaceas do not work in the long run.

5. Get a checkup and take medicine as prescribed. If you have any kind of physical issues, even small ones, make sure to attend to them.

6. Go to the dentist. This is probably the last place you want to be right now, but having nice, healthy teeth is very important for overall well-being.

Changes to your exterior can make a big difference in how you feel too. Buy new clothes, get a haircut, and do things that show the world that you are changing inside and out. When you reward yourself for the work you are doing, make sure the reward includes some treats for your external self like expensive shampoo or special cologne. Observe yourself in a mirror and affirm that you are fabulous and that anyone in his or her right mind would want you. Keep yourself looking strong, healthy, and happy, and soon you'll feel strong, healthy, and happy.

The "Date Night"

Absolutely essential to your self-care routine is that you spend one night each week with yourself—I call this "date night," or "me time." One of the most therapeutic things you can do for yourself is to make the effort to spend time with you. It is critical that you begin to know and value yourself, and you do that by spending time alone, doing nice things for yourself. Your date night solidifies and symbolizes your commitment to yourself. It doesn't have to be a night—it could be a weekend morning—but it does have to be uninterrupted time alone that you have planned out and given some thought to.

During your date night, turn off the phone, the computer, and anything else that would allow someone to get in touch with you. If you have children, have your date night after they go to bed or on the weekends before they get up, but be sure to have it. Don't let taking care of others be an excuse not to take care of yourself.

When my own therapist first suggested this, I hadn't catered to myself or spent time with myself in years. When I first started, I felt guilty. But I picked a night anyway, and after I put my kids to bed, I would turn off the phone. That was also hard for me, because my friends had been my salvation since my breakup. I did it, though, because I knew that I would never be okay if I didn't learn how to be alone.

At first it felt strange and not very nice. I thought it signaled that my life was dull, boring, and lonely. But my therapist cautioned me to "make peace with the peace" and see the solitude as regenerative and the alone time necessary to get in touch with who I am and what I want. As uncomfortable as it was, I started out just taking a long bubble bath, deep-conditioning my hair, and climbing into bed with a good novel. But as the weeks went on I not only looked forward to this time alone, but I started to shop for it. At first I could only "splurge" on some nice, scented bath salts, but after a while I bought expensive conditioner, then designer pajamas, and finally luxurious sheets, pillows, and down comforters. As I added to my repertoire, I began to feel truly pampered, and soon I looked forward to my date night and would be very cranky if something prevented me from having it.

In the spring and summer, I took long bike rides on Sunday mornings. Admittedly, sometimes these rides were lonely and, again, I struggled to make peace with the peace, but still I rode every Sunday. I learned to be alone, to sit and watch the world go by. Many times my grief came up and I felt sad, but I was working things out in my head and getting my body in shape. So I remained dedicated to riding.

A friend of mine took a woodworking class because it was something he had always wanted to do. He started out small but eventually bought some nice tools and turned an area of his home into a woodshop. After that, he started to spend time each Sunday working in his woodshop making nice things for himself. Now he's in a relationship with a woman who has children, so he has to be more flexible with his Sundays. But he still knows that it's important to spend alone time both in and out of a relationship. He's changed his "me time" to Thursday, and still keeps the commitment to himself every week.

Do nice things for yourself and reward yourself for doing the difficult work—and do it consistently. If you need to relax, do that; if it makes you feel better to be active, do that. But whatever activity you decide to do, schedule a "me" night at least once a week and stay committed to it.

Some of my reader and client suggestions include

taking yourself shopping;
buying a new book;
taking a bubble bath;
going to or renting a movie;
playing a rousing game of golf, pool, basketball, or racquetball;
taking a long bike ride;
deep-conditioning your hair;
getting a massage;
getting your nails done;
taking yourself to dinner;
sitting in the park and reading a book;
going for a long walk along a scenic path;
taking your camera out and shooting photos; and
booking a spa day.

There is a tremendous payoff to learning to spend time doing good things for yourself. Not only will it make you feel better, but you will attract other positive people who know that self-care is a priority.

Therapy and Support Groups

No one wants to go through a difficult time alone. Friends are great, but don't overlook the power of a therapist to make this time easier. A good therapist can be your confidant, your support system, your guide, and your biggest cheerleader. How do you find a good therapist? It might take a few meetings with two or three to find the right one for you, but trust that the right one is out there.

Don't go with the first therapist you pick out of a phone book. First you want to find out what kind of training they've had. Is there something they specialize in? Is there a certain type of client their practice is geared toward? For instance, if you are doing deep grief work you don't want to go to a behavioral therapist who specializes in phobias because grief work is not a phobia and a change in behavior will not help very much. If you want to explore family dynamics, it's important to find a therapist who will do that with you. Many therapists will take you on even if you have a different opinion than they do as to what you need for effective therapy. The therapist will think that he or she knows what is best for you, but that is not always the case.

Look them up on the Internet or call several therapists to ask what type of therapy they practice and who makes up their main client base. Even if you don't understand what they say in response, take notes and then research the answer to see if this fits with your needs. Go in person to interview two or three therapists to see if you're comfortable. Your interview process with potential therapists is about finding a good therapist for you. Do not worry about hurting the therapist's feelings. A good therapist will encourage you to shop around.

In addition to a therapist, you might want to find support groups. These can be twelve-step programs or community groups. Depending on where you live, there may be many different groups to choose from. In journaling and writing your inventories, you may find that you're dealing with issues like alcoholism, addiction, trauma, abuse, or mental illness, whether yours or someone else's. If so, support groups abound, and you may find it helpful to be around others who are going through similar experiences. If your ex-partner was the one with an alcohol or drug addiction, sex addiction, or any other addiction that was a problem in your past relationship, you might want to go to Co-dependents Anonymous, Emotions Anonymous, Al-Anon, Nar-Anon, or COSLAA.

Attending twelve-step groups can be a source of inspiration and support for you. If you go to a meeting and don't like it, try out a different group, and if you don't like that one, try a third. If you don't like three in a row, journal about what is going on to figure out whether the problem comes from within you.

Social and Recreational Groups

If you're coming out of a long relationship or have gone from relationship to relationship without a break in-between, you might discover that you no longer have many outside interests. You need to start cultivating them from the beginning of your breakup. Doing this will not only make the breakup a smoother transition for you, but it will give you ways to meet new people, express yourself, and discover new aspects of your personality.

A hobby, sports, or social group can be a great way to meet people with similar interests to yours. Joining these types of groups is not the same as just keeping busy. This exploration is an important step in the rebuilding process because it's about rediscovering who you are, and discovering that there are other people like you out there.

At first it may be tough to get out because you feel too raw and introverted to start looking for groups that fit your interests. Give yourself the time you need, but once you feel ready, find things you enjoy and people you want to be around. Investigate a few options that get you out and about, and see what you like. Even then, when you do decide to venture out, it might be difficult to let go, have fun, and not be self-conscious. Your affirmations will help with this as time goes by. Keep trying.

If you do want to join groups right away, that's great. Just don't get so busy that your work falls by the wayside. Remember, your goal is balance. Don't fall too deeply into your new social network, and don't stay isolated, either.

You may have found some new interests when you were retraining your brain, but branch out even further to increase your social network. Look into church groups, reading groups, softball teams, bowling leagues. Join a gym and take some classes there. Take informal classes at a community college. If you want to learn to play golf or some other sport, there are probably clinics you can attend. If you've always wanted to act, join a community theater group. If you've always wanted to sing, join a choir or other singing group. Go to Meetup.com and find other groups that regularly get together in person. It's important to socialize, in person, with new people.

Support is important, groups are important, and building your life is important. Without self-care and paying attention to yourself and your wants and needs, it becomes easier to slip back into a relationship before you are ready or to contact your ex and play games on that front. Making yourself a priority in your life helps with the work you must do and builds a foundation for your future. When you make your life a priority, it sends a message to healthy people who are attracted to those with rich, full lives. Take care of your life and your life will take care of you.

5

Seven Rules for Making Things Easier for Your Children

"I have no idea how to explain this all to my kids."

"My ex-husband has inappropriate relationships with inappropriate women. We've been divorced four years and he won't listen when I tell him these women are unhealthy."

"My kids despise their stepfather and I've tried to talk to my ex-wife about his 'discipline' of them, but she defends everything he does."

"My kids object to my dating, so I don't let them know when I'm going out with a woman. They ask and I lie about it. Basically, I'm sneaking around on them."

"When my marriage ended, I felt lost and alone. Just caring for [my kids'] physical and logistical needs was a chore, but I could

> not deal with the pain in their eyes. As a result, I lost complete control over them and each of them started getting in trouble. It was a tide I could not stem and eventually my ex took custody and control."

A breakup, never an easy experience in the first place, becomes even more difficult and complicated when children are involved. Children carry their own burdens about the breakup and sometimes express their feelings by acting out. They don't want their parents to split up, and are hurt and confused about what's going on. Behavior problems can surface in normally well-behaved kids, or become worse in kids who already have behavior problems. Some children respond to their parents' breakup by becoming shy and awkward; others become loud and obnoxious. No matter how they show their feelings outwardly, every child will have emotions about the breakup. Dealing with a child's feelings becomes an additional challenge for a parent dealing with his or her own breakup trauma and the new logistics of being a single parent. But as difficult and often overwhelming as it may seem at first, it is possible to be a happy and healthy family in the aftermath of a breakup.

At the very core of every child whose parents are breaking up is a primal fear of "What's going to happen to me?" Children personalize the world around them and don't understand that the breakup is not about them. Even when they are unconditionally cared for and considered by two loving, giving parents, children still feel the loss of the family unit.

It is important to take your child's well-being into consideration while still being a firm and guiding parent. Children need you to be strong and they rely on your good judgment to help them navigate the scary and difficult post-"my-parents-are-divorcing" world. Here are seven rules to follow so that your children feel secure and cared for:

1. Be open with your children about the breakup.

Talk to the children. Sit them down and gently tell them that what is going on is not about them, and that Mom and Dad still love them no matter what. If they ask about what went wrong, don't give specifics but keep your response in broad terms, such as, "Mom and Dad cannot live together peacefully, and everyone deserves to live in a peaceful home." If the children are older, this is a good time to talk about the importance of making good choices in life. Impress upon your children—again using broad language—that when a situation is no longer healthy, it has to change. Try to give your kids something to hold onto for their own future relationships.

Your children may need time to process what you are saying, so don't expect a response. Let them know you are there if they need to talk and also offer to get them a counselor if they want to talk to someone else. On the other hand, there is a chance they will have a response, so be prepared. They may have a lot of questions that really have no answers such as, "Why can't you two just get along?" Let the kids know that you tried and sometimes these things happen and no one is at fault. If a child has an intense reaction to your news, allow the child to express these emotions without taking them personally. Keep your child safe and do not allow physical violence or self-harm. If the reaction seems too extreme to you, seek the help of a professional.

Don't wait for a child's "blessing" or some kind of reassurance from the child that he or she understands why this needs to happen. This talk is not about assuaging your guilt, but about letting the children know that their thoughts and emotions are okay and that you welcome the chance to share them and talk about them, even if those thoughts and feelings are negative or difficult.

During the "we're breaking up" talk, stress how much you love them and that even if you seem distracted in the days and weeks ahead, you are always there for them.

2. Monitor yourself and model healthy behavior.

Watch what you say and do around your children. Kids know more than they let on, and understand more than you think. When adults are not getting along, children are sensitive to changes in the environment. Be careful about what you say, even if they're not in the room or you don't think they are listening. Don't try to use euphemisms that you think will go over their heads, either. Even if they don't let on, they may well understand and they are definitely watching and taking it all in. Therefore, model healthy behavior for your children by acting in the ways you want them to act. Show them what self-respect, self-discipline, healthy communication, boundaries, and value systems look like.

When someone moves out, the remaining family is a "new" family. Becoming a new family is an opportunity to make healthy changes around the house. Strengthen your family bond by asking the children for input into "new" family rules and procedures. Keep your household organized because it assures children that their world is secure and orderly. Many a harried single parent falls into a trap of either yelling and barking orders or letting it all fall apart. Instead, sit down and talk about the new family and how everyone needs to step up to the plate and help out. Talk about how to handle outings, meals, and chores. Make sure all your kids are participating by helping you shop or planning menus. Come up with ideas—as a family—for fun things you can do together as a reward for helping the household run efficiently.

Remember to reinforce your kids' positive behavior rather than just punishing. Notice when a child is helping out or modeling good behavior and say "thank you." Give encouragement when you notice that your child has improved his or her behavior, even if the improvement is small. My middle son would always eat with his fingers even though he was constantly told not to. Whenever I noticed him with a fork I would thank him for using a fork. Noticing the little things takes work, especially if you are caught up in your own pain. But it's important to recognize small strides that children make, and to remember to praise things they're "supposed" to be doing. Get into the habit of looking for things they do without your having to ask, and use encouraging phrases like "I knew you could do it!", "You're doing so well!" or "Thank you for being such a helper." Pour on the encouragement and they will respond to it, as long as you're recognizing genuine effort by showing genuine appreciation. Thank them, often, for the role they're taking and the responsibilities they're taking on in the new family.

3. Remember that your ex is still your child's parent.

When a breakup occurs, many parents put their children in the middle, whether unwittingly or on purpose. One woman, an only child growing up, said to me, "My parents were very angry with each other after the divorce. My mother would say horrible things about my dad to me, and my dad would do the same [about my mother]. I was five years old when it all started, and it went on for years." This woman attributed all of the interpersonal struggles she had had since then, both with her parents and in romantic relationships, to her parents' breakup acrimony.

Develop your post-breakup relationship with your ex like you would a business relationship. Treat your ex like a business partner and keep personal exchanges out of it. Be civil to your ex in front of the children, and don't bad-mouth your ex or use your child as a sounding board about him or her. If you have visitation issues, discuss them away from the children. If your ex is truly intolerable, try to find some middle ground where you can agree on how visitation exchanges happen. If you need court intervention, ask for it rather than trying to enforce visitation or support orders yourself.

Don't get into game playing with your ex. Yes, you're probably very angry, and maybe there's nothing you would love more than to get back at that bleeping so-and-so. But don't do it because, if you do, it will hurt your children. Stop all the nonsense. If you have unfinished business, take it to a therapist—not to your ex—and especially not in front of the kids. Don't say things in front of the kids or to the kids in hopes that it will find its way back to your ex. That is manipulative behavior, and it's not okay.

It is very important to choose your battles carefully. Do not fight every week about every little thing. You are going to need to learn to let some things go. On the other hand, if your ex is the one who does not know what this means, there are times you are going to have to cut the conversation off. Make it clear that you will not fight about small things that do not matter.

At the same time, though, if something really needs attention, both parents should talk about it. This doesn't mean the stepparents or the new boyfriend and girlfriend; it means the parents. Do not let your current partner or your ex's current partner get involved in these discussions. These are your children and the two of you need to learn to talk about issues that come up with them without interference. If the issues come up when it's not a convenient time to talk, set up another time. Choose your battles wisely, but don't let the important ones go.

Do not confuse the children by allowing your ex to come and go in your house. A good relationship with a co-parent is great, but don't give up your privacy or your separateness in the name of good cheer among everyone. You have to show your children what "moving on" is all about—being happy, healthy, and whole—which starts with having good, clear boundaries and separate lives.

4. Wait to introduce your children to new partners.

It is very difficult for children to see their parents with new people. It takes a while for kids to adjust to a world in which their parents are no longer together, so it's never a good idea to force them to adjust to someone else right away.

People frequently ask me for a time frame for introducing a serious relationship to the children. It's always hard to say, but I usually suggest at least a year from the time you and your ex separate for younger children, and six months to a year for older children. To you this may seem like a long time, but to them it's not. Your children need time to process your separation, and then have you to themselves for a while, and then get used to your involvement with someone new. Individual differences in your kids and in your situation may mean that they'll need even more time. Everyone is different and adjusts to new situations at different rates. You can't force your children to accept someone new, and it will be easier for everyone if you wait a while.

Immediately after your breakup, it's important to spend some time alone to do your grief work and start building your own life. Dating right away is not advisable. However, some people feel as if they've done their grieving while still in a dying relationship and are anxious to get back out there once their breakup or divorce is official. One woman said to me, "I've been in a loveless marriage for so long and can't wait to date." Although that was true for her, her kids were not aware that she was in a loveless marriage, and when she immediately started dating, it was hard for them to handle. Take it slow, and when you do first start dating, it is not necessary to share this with your children.

Besides making the transition into a new relationship easier for your kids, another reason for taking your time is that if the relationship does become serious, it will help the later formation of a family unit. Pushing your kids to accept someone new before they've had time to process your breakup can set you up for failure. When children resent a new partner because he or she came on the scene too quickly, that is a hurdle that may never be overcome. While some kids are going to resist new partners no matter what you do, keeping your side of the street clean by introducing someone gradually will do much to ensure that the children do eventually accept this new person as part of their lives.

When you do get involved with someone, let your new partner know that your children are your first priority. Encourage your kids to be open with you when you become involved with someone new. Let them know their opinions matter. It's important that they know they can have input. Ultimately, who you become involved with and how you run your family is your choice and your business. Striking a balance between these two messages is difficult, but it's one you must strive for.

In one of my seminars, a woman shared that her ten-year-old daughter told her she could never remarry. She laughed, finding it amusing. In this situation, though, a child needs to be told that although she is the most important consideration and her opinions are important, it's not her choice whether or not her parent remarries.

Another woman, long divorced, said she stopped dating because every time she brought someone home, the children would make rude comments, and when she didn't bring her partners home the children would tell her that they didn't like her dating. Instead of giving up on dating, which reinforced the children's negative behavior, she needed to set boundaries and act like a parent who is entitled to a nice life, including being able to date. Remember, monitor and model. This includes not being a martyr for the kids or allowing them to run your love life. That is not model behavior because it's not the way you want your own kids to lead their lives when they're adults.

It's important to tell your children that there are positive aspects to a breakup and that making difficult choices is better than staying in a bad relationship, so make sure your new relationship is a healthy model. Show your children that you will not have anyone in your life who does not respect you and them. Cast the breakup as a positive, life-affirming choice and show your kids that you are in charge of your own life by choosing healthy new partners.

When Your Ex Becomes Involved with Another Person

You can shout the "should"s and guidelines from the rooftop, but that does not mean your ex is going to follow them. If your ex fails to understand that it's not a good idea to bring new boyfriends or girlfriends around the kids, you may need to take further action early in a separation by asking the court for an order stating that no unrelated males or females can be around the children. This will usually stay in place until the divorce is final, but after the divorce is final, there is not much you can do.

If your ex's choices in new mates are questionable, try not to become overly involved in it. Guide the children and give them the sense that they can talk to you, but don't run back to your ex barking ultimatums because the kids hate the new person. Try to give guidance to the children while practicing a hands-off approach with your ex. In most cases, everyone's lives will be saner. Remember, monitor and model.

While it can be a challenge when your ex is bringing home people who are not the best role models for your kids, the situation can be even worse when an ex moves on to a new partner who is great and gets along well with your kids. One woman said,

> The difficult part that I was not expecting was hearing about how wonderfully the new girlfriend can cook, how much fun they all had making lasagna from scratch. [It's difficult] knowing that they are doing the same "family" [activities] we enjoyed while married, including [going to the same] vacation places. While I have struggled to find someone up to my standards to date, there he is in a long-term relationship within weeks of the divorce being final. It is not at all that I want the ex back, but I am jealous of the "family" time the new girlfriend gets that I have lost.

Another man said, "I did not expect my ex-wife's boyfriend to teach the kids how to play sports and to be actively involved with them. He's even coaching one of the teams! He's a great guy, but sometimes I can't stand how great he is." Without a doubt, it's difficult when your ex and his or her new partner are ready to be a family and you're still sorting out being single. However, it's not a reflection on you, so try not to take it to heart. Doing your grief and healing work is important, as is building a life alone right now. Try to be grateful that your ex has someone who cares about your kids and know that it doesn't replace what you are to them unless you let it. If you're the noncustodial parent, stay close to your children and stay involved in their lives. Don't just think someone else has it covered, because they need you no matter how great your ex's new partner may be. Spend time with your kids and let them know you care.

Even in the most perfect blended families, problems can and do occur. Sometimes the problems are with an ex and sometimes they are with an ex's partner. If the children talk to you about a problem that's going on, try to talk them through the situation before going to your ex. It's almost always a losing battle to argue with your ex about the kids and the new partner. Try to address it with the kids first, and find solutions together.

If children are having issues with their noncustodial parent and his or her new love, try to help by suggesting different ways of approaching the problem. Encourage the kids to tough out any situation that doesn't compromise their health or safety, and to be as respectful as possible when visiting. It might be difficult to teach your children how to be polite and communicate in a healthy way with someone who appears to be doing wrong, but teach your children that it's important to keep their side of the street clean no matter what someone else is doing. This is a life lesson that comes in handy no matter what the situation, and this can be a great opportunity to teach it.

Your job is to protect your children, and sometimes the best way to do this is by teaching them to protect themselves. With older children and teenagers this is especially important because it's easy to blame a teenager for whatever issues arise. When teenagers are sullen and difficult, it is easy to say the problem lies with them, but this is not always the case. Teaching your kids to be respectful and to use healthy communication will keep them from becoming scapegoats or from being identified as the source of the problem when they're not. Teach them to use "I" language, as in "I feel . . ." and "I think . . . ," and to be specific about what they're feeling or thinking. For example, instead of saying to their father, "You always pay more attention to Kathie and her kids than you do to me," your kids can learn from you to say, "I feel hurt when I come to visit with you and I don't feel I have your attention." If the parent goes on the defensive or is dismissive (saying something like "You do have my attention!"), an older child or teenager can learn to say, "I feel hurt that Kathie's kids live with you and see you all the time and I don't. When I come here, I'd like to spend some time alone with you." Also teach them to ask, specifically, for what they want. "I'd like to go to the movies, just you and me (or you, me, and my siblings)."

It is also helpful to let your children know that sometimes no matter how clear their communication is, the other parent may give them no response or a negative response. Remind them it's important that they do their best to try to make an important relationship work out. It's good when a parent hears you when you're trying to communicate something, but sometimes he or she won't. Let your children know it's not their fault if this happens. If you think you need to intervene at this time, you might try talking to your ex, but if the children didn't get anywhere, chances are you won't either. Remember—choose your battles wisely.

5. Give and get child support.

If you are the noncustodial parent, pay your child support and don't think for a minute that it's too much. It's not. While there are rare cases where the noncustodial parent is giving too much, usually your support is not 50 percent of what it takes to raise your child. If your ex is playing games by hiding income or inflating expenses, go through the courts for help. Do not try to resolve this on your own, and do not involve the children in it.

Likewise, if you are the custodial parent, make sure you get what you deserve. Do not let the other parent off the hook by not asking for child support. This is not your money; it is your kids' money, so fight for it. At the same time, though, do not try to get more than you are entitled to. Share the financial responsibility.

The issue of child support would be less antagonistic if everyone realized that being honest, and giving and getting your fair share, is in the children's best interest. If the other parent thinks you are taking advantage of him or her, this animosity is going to spill over into the relationship with the children, and no one will win. Don't play games with child support, no matter what side you are on. If the other side insists on doing so, document everything and then ask a lawyer for a consultation or see a family-law facilitator if your jurisdiction has one. They will best advise you what to do.

6. Continue to be a parent to your children.

Every week I receive e-mail from newly single parents complaining that their children are out of control or that they've allowed the children to disrespect or take advantage of them. Not only do children need you to be a parent, they want you to be a parent.

If your children are misbehaving, think about how you can change the way you are doing things and what you are modeling for them. Listen to the way you talk, how you are behaving toward them, and the boundaries and limits you are setting for them. Have your actions and expectations been unclear? Have you backpedaled on your decisions? Are you sending mixed messages to your kids? Have you become more lenient with them because their other parent is too strict in your view? If you answered "yes" to any of these questions, you need to review and revise your approach to parenting.

After a breakup, children can act out and often misbehave in ways they did not before the split. A guilty parent will sometimes back away from discipline. It seems contrary to the nature of a loving parent to become stricter with kids after a breakup, but that is often what they need. They need to know you are in charge and you are capable.

While children always need guidelines and limits, these are especially important in the aftermath of a breakup. Your children will never tell you this, because it's not something they are consciously aware of, but limits and boundaries make them feel secure. By giving them boundaries, you are letting them know the parameters of their world, and you are letting them know you are in charge. You are there to protect them. If you let them ride roughshod over you, how can you protect them from someone much bigger and stronger down the road? They need to know you can and will protect them from the difficult things in the world.

Therefore, it's important to show the children you are strong and can keep order in their world. Set limits and boundaries for them, and do not allow these limits and boundaries to be compromised. Sometimes the most loving thing you can say to your kids is "no." It's easy to understand how during tough times, parents will sometimes soften up out of guilt or from thinking that the children are too vulnerable or fragile to be told a firm "no." No means no. It does not mean yes, and don't let it turn into yes. Remember, you need to show your kids you can keep them safe from the big bad outside world. If you're a pushover, you're not showing them that. You're the parent. Act like one.

Set goals, limits, and expectations, then enforce them. Assign chores and give responsibilities. Make sure that children know who owns what and who is responsible for what. A child without limits does not know how to make choices or how to consider others' feelings, thoughts, and personal space. No matter how hurt or angry your children are, you must insist that they treat you with respect. This teaches them that even when life is difficult, there is no excuse for behaving badly. At the same time, make sure the children know they are entitled to all of their feelings. It is okay to have negative feelings, but it is not okay to act out on them or act inappropriately.

Logical and Natural Consequences

Children need to know that there are consequences for their actions. Your children should experience two types of consequences: natural and logical. Natural consequences are the natural results of adverse actions. For example, if a child does not eat, he or she goes hungry. If a child doesn't wake up on time, he or she has to walk to school. If a child refuses to wear a hat, he or she will get cold. If a child leaves toys out in the rain, the toys rust. These are natural consequences for doing or failing to do something.

Let your children suffer the natural consequences of their behavior. Don't interfere. Don't coddle and do things to prevent these consequences for your children—like driving your son to school after a missed school bus, or making a special meal if your daughter refuses to eat what you've offered. Also don't nag or yell about what your kids need to do differently. Just let nature take its course. If a child forgets her schoolbooks at home, the natural consequence is that the teacher gets upset or the child's grade is impacted. The solution is *not* for Mom or Dad to drive the books to school. Allowing natural consequences to happen teaches children that they need to be responsible. This is a lesson that will continue into adulthood. If your children learn now, they will be healthier and feel more capable and, therefore, pick healthy, capable partners.

Logical consequences, on the other hand, are reasonably and logically related to the offense, but don't occur naturally. In other words, you must enforce consequences for the behavior you're trying to change. If a child doesn't eat dinner, the parent can decide that he or she doesn't get dessert. If a child persists in leaving things all over the house, the parent can say, "If I have to pick up your things, I'm putting them away for a few days and you won't be able to have them." Alternately, the parent could say, "You cannot watch television until the toys are picked up." That way, the child chooses how long the consequence will be enforced.

It is always good to give options and allow children to make the choice because it helps kids to focus. For example, if children are wrestling in the house you can say, "You boys can play with toys in here, or you can wrestle outside. What's it going to be?" This is much more effective than screaming at them to "Stop that now!"

Natural and logical consequences work very well for modifying children's behavior, but you have to provide these consequences or allow them to happen, and you have to do it all the time.

Boundaries and the Three-Times Rule

A student of mine came to me with the following problem with her son, Ethan, who is four years old. One rainy day he said to his mother, "I want to go out." Mother said, "No, it's raining, you can't go out today." Ethan said, "I want to go out." Mother said, "It's raining, we're not going outside today." At that point Ethan threw himself to the floor, screaming that he wanted to go out. His mother dressed them in rain gear, and they went out.

Ethan won by behaving badly, so his negative behavior was reinforced. Ethan now knows that a tantrum gets him what he wants. His mother obviously needs boundaries, but she said to me, "Oh, I can't stand to see him like this." Parenting 101 is that you have to be able to stand to see him like this, because he's four and his parent needs to send a message that negative behavior does not get rewarded.

I explained to her that she needs to let him have his tantrum until he exhausts himself. He can either stay where he is, or she can pick him up, without words and without anger, and place him on his bed until he stops. If he gets up while he is still having his tantrum, she can bring him back to his bed until he stops. If she knows from the start that she can't keep picking him up and bringing him back, she needs to just let him have his tantrum where he is. When he gets no payoff for his negative behavior, the behavior will stop.

This mother had the same problem at the store when Ethan wanted a new toy. At the store, he snatched toy after toy from the shelves. She grabbed his hands and put everything back on the shelves. He became frustrated and threw himself on the floor. She capitulated and bought him a toy. Again, the four-year-old won.

I told her to wordlessly pick Ethan up and leave the store, leaving behind the shopping cart and everything she had in it. Go sit in the car and tell him, "When you are done, we will return to the store." Once he finishes thrashing about, they can go back inside. If he starts up again, they go back out to the car. On the third time out to the car, they go home. It is very important that on the third time, they cancel the trip completely and go home.

If you've ever wondered why some children behave in stores and others don't, this is why. When in a store with a misbehaving child, do not get angry, do not give in to their demands, do not try to placate them with treats and bribes. Just let them know who is in charge and where your boundaries are. The rule is: I take you to the store and you behave. End of story.

Is this type of "training" time-consuming? Yes. Does it work? Yes. You won't have to do this forever. Once your children know that you say what you mean and mean what you say, the negative behavior will stop. Eventually Ethan's mother will be able to say, "If you touch one more toy, or ask for something, we're going in the car and going home." Ethan will know she means it because it's what she has always done. When you set boundaries in a clear and consistent way, people get it. Kids, especially, are quick learners. It may take more work up front, but in the long run it's less. Do the tough work up front and life will get easier and stay easier. When kids become teenagers they have to know that you say what you mean and mean what you say. If you start when they're four, their teenage years will be much easier on everyone.

Consistency is extremely important in setting boundaries. Another client of mine was in a restaurant with her three children, ages seven, nine, and eleven. They ordered and the waiter brought drinks, but the kids would not settle down. Their mother told them to stop, and they would stop for a minute and then start up again. It was clear that their unruly behavior was disturbing other diners. Their mother said, for the last time, that if they continued, they were going home. The children continued to misbehave.

Mother signaled the waiter to pay for the drinks and they started to leave. The kids did not want to go, and started to promise that they would be good. But the mother refused to change her mind. She had given them three chances, she said, and they had not behaved. The youngest child started to cry; he actually sat down on the floor and said he wasn't leaving. The entire restaurant was looking at them. Thinking about what we'd talked about, she simply took him by the wrist, again not angry, and walked him out. He flailed and tried to throw himself on the floor, so she picked him up, sternly but wordlessly, took them out to the car, and they went home. On the way home she reminded them that if they cannot behave in public, then they cannot go out in public. The next time they went out to a restaurant, the kids began to fool around again. Once she reminded them that they will go home if they continue, though, they stopped and stayed stopped. This time, they believed her.

Is this hard? Yes, it's very hard for a parent to leave a restaurant with three children. But it's even harder for a parent to sit there while three children misbehave dinner after dinner. You remove them a couple of times and you will never have to do it again.

Some parents might need to do this a few times, but the children will eventually get the idea, and after that they will always behave in restaurants. This good behavior will last a parent for years, and all he or she has had to do is leave a restaurant a few times. It's tough in the beginning, but it has a lasting effect.

Giving children a three-times rule is important. When you give the second warning, say, "If I have to say this one more time, we're going home." Kids respond to this because they like to know where the limits are. If the negative behavior happens three times, it is time to act.

7. Children always appreciate quality time.

Spend time with your children, both individually and as a group if you have more than one. This is especially important after you start introducing a new partner into their lives. If you become seriously involved with someone who has children too, do not force your children to like the other children; even if your kids and your partner's kids like each other, be sure to take time with just your kids. Find out what each child likes to do most, and make an evening or day out of it. Make sure your children know they're special, and treat each one like he or she is special, separate and apart from his or her siblings as well. Spending time with each child reassures them and creates a special bond for life. It doesn't have to be anything extravagant. It can be a matter of going to the movies or out to dinner or renting a movie. The important thing is to make sure your children know that you care about them and their interests, and that you're there for them. Encourage your children. Make sure you are boosting their self-esteem and being their biggest cheerleader. Say "I love you" and give hugs a lot. You might think that your kids know that you're a loving and devoted parent, but during a tumultuous transition like this they need to hear you say the words—repeatedly, over an extended period of time.

Parenting Is Tough: Ask for Help

Ask for help when you need it. If you need to take a parenting class, don't be embarrassed. If you need to see a therapist to learn how to parent or resolve some of the issues you're facing, do it. Buy parenting books and participate in forums on parenting Web sites. This is new territory for your whole family, so there's nothing wrong with not knowing how to act. Your kids will be better off if you take the time to learn to do it right.

Above all else, remember that your kids really didn't ask to be born. You made that decision. Be responsible about that, and have compassion about what they're going through even though it's a rough time for you, too. As a family, all of you will get through this. You may even come out stronger people as a result.

6

Bringing the Big Picture into Focus: The Relationship and Life Inventories

In this chapter you will do the important work of understanding not only your last relationship, but also the recurring patterns in your life. The inventories are integral to moving on, finishing your unfinished business, and preparing for your next relationship.

Although everything you'll need is here, please don't think that you have to do everything in this chapter before moving on to the next—in fact, that's not even advisable. The work in this chapter could last months. Take your time and work with a therapist or support group, or incorporate the inventories into your nightly journaling. Return to this chapter as necessary, but don't get stuck here. And remember to balance this essential work with plenty of self-care.

The Relationship Inventory

"It was not until I did the Relationship Inventory that I was able to honestly see the relationship for what it was. In my mind what we had was so good and I struggled to let it go. Once the Relationship Inventory put things into perspective, it was so much easier to move forward."

"Doing the Relationship Inventory grounded me. I stopped wistfully remembering the happy times and was able to look [at] how it really was."

"We had been broken up [for] months. I felt stuck and thought I was never going to get over it. I figured I would try the Relationship Inventory but didn't expect much. I read through it and then quickly jotted down ten things that were positive and ten things that were negative. Suddenly I was reeling because it felt so intense. In all those months since the breakup, I had never looked honestly at the relationship. I had just been moping around remembering things very selectively. Doing the Relationship Inventory is what finally put me on the road to healing."

"I started doing the Relationship Inventory and it works! I feel lighter already!"

"The 'red flag' portion of the Relationship Inventory really helped me. I could not believe how many there were. When I started dating again I was able to end several liaisons because I was able to recognize the red flags. I finally had control of my life."

"The Relationship Inventory was a life-changing and eye-opening experience for me. I started inventorying every failed relationship I've ever had and in doing so I realized that I had a definite pattern. I also realized I had a lot of unresolved grief and rage inside of me. I was always one of those people who said everything was fine when under it all, nothing was."

"I found the letter exercise extremely helpful. I wrote letters to every guy I ever dated as well as to dysfunctional members of my family who had mistreated me. I read all of them out loud, burned them, cried, and then I felt a lot better."

"You can't avoid the land mines if you don't know where they are. The Relationship Inventory exercise helped me map out my land mines and now I have a real chance to avoid them as I move forward."

Often, when people are grieving, they tend to view their former relationship in a light that doesn't accurately reflect reality. Remembering certain parts and forgetting other parts is called "splitting." We compartmentalize the good parts and bad parts and only revisit the parts we want to. Splitting allows us to become lost in, and controlled by, our emotions and our fantasies. Extreme views cause us to lose perspective and remain in either anger or sorrow. To truly move forward, we must assess our relationship for what it really was.

While everyone loses some perspective after a breakup, the relationship cannot truly be grieved unless it is seen for what it was. The purpose of the Relationship Inventory is to take you out of the emotion and the fantasy and into the objective and the realistic. That is not to say that you won't have any emotions as you write the Relationship Inventory—you certainly will—but the exercise will keep you in check and on task despite your emotions. The Relationship Inventory will help you control your thoughts and feelings instead of allowing them to control you.

The Relationship Inventory moves you further along in getting over it, both emotionally and cognitively. By taking a step back and evaluating the relationship, you will not only stop splitting, which will help you with the emotional healing, but you will come to understand, cognitively and rationally, how things really were in the relationship.

You can do the steps in any order, or even do a little of each step every day. However, I've found that sometimes it's easier to concentrate on one step at a time while remaining aware of the others—this way, if something comes to you while you are journaling, talking to a friend, or in a therapy session, you can write it down. If you become overwhelmed, stop, take a break, and do your self-caring exercises.

How you write your inventory is up to you, but do try to take your time. You want your inventory to be as comprehensive as possible, but not so difficult you can't complete it. One inventory should take no less than a week and no more than a couple of weeks to do. Get the job done, but be gentle with yourself along the way.

Writing the Relationship Inventory

1. Make a list of all the positive things about the relationship. Note that you're not listing the positive things about your ex

(that comes later), but the positive things about that particular relationship (e.g., you liked having a boy/girlfriend, you liked going to your ex's parents' house for Sunday dinner, you liked your ex's friends, you liked going somewhere your ex took you regularly where you had never been before).

2. Make a list of all the positive qualities of your ex. Write down all the traits that you liked and that were important to you.
3. Write down five special things your ex did for you or five special times during the relationship.
4. Make a list of things that your friends and family liked about your ex. Were they the same things you liked about your ex?
5. Make a list of the things you liked about your ex that your friends or family did not like. What kinds of things put you at odds with friends or family? Do you feel your ex was misunderstood, or did you suspect that your family and friends were right? Did you explain or excuse the behavior that others did not like in your ex?
6. Make a list of all the negative things about the relationship. Again, this is not the negative things about your ex, but the negative things unique to that particular relationship (e.g., you couldn't go out with your friends when you wanted to, you had to let your ex know when you were home).
7. Make a list of all of your ex's negative qualities. Focus on aspects of your ex that you really disliked and wanted to change.
8. Make a list of all the positive qualities that turned into negative qualities for you over time. For example, maybe you were initially impressed that this person was very neat and

clean, but later he or she berated you for your lack of neatness. Perhaps you were drawn to this person because of financial stability and later realized it was actually unreasonable frugality. Perhaps you initially thought this person to be confident and assertive but eventually recognized him or her as controlling and inflexible. Think about things that drew you in, but that you wound up disliking or seeing differently by the end.

9. Think back to the beginning of the relationship and make a list of all the early warning signs. Did you have an argument early on, or was there some behavior that gave you a clue that this was not going to work out—maybe something that gave you a hint that this person was capable of hurting you deeply? What warning signs were flashing loud and clear? What did you do about it? What did you not do about it? How did you manage to rationalize it to yourself, or did you just ignore it completely? What could you have done about it way back when? Why didn't you? What compromises or bargains did you make with yourself? What price did you pay for those compromises?
10. Write down the five most hurtful incidents to you in the relationship. What was done? What was said? Was there an apology or a reassurance that it would never happen again? Did it happen again? Were there apologies and promises made and not kept?
11. Write down the things you feel you did wrong (not what your ex said you did wrong but what you truly feel you did wrong). Include both things you did and things you didn't do. Write about everything you can think of—not speaking

to your ex, being controlling, being in a bad mood, picking a fight, or bringing up issues that weren't important.

12. Write down any major incidents or issues in the relationship that stemmed from your own issues or your own behavior. Was there something you did that led to a major blowup? Write down anything that you would take back if you could.
13. Write down any significant statements you would have liked to say. What has gone unsaid? If you had your ex in a room for five minutes and he or she could not respond, what would you say? This is your opportunity to say whatever needs to be said that does not fall into numbers 1 to 12.

Write your answers over the course of a week or two and then take a two- or three-day break. During the break, don't look at the inventories or do any kind of work. This break is very important and these days are for you to relax, have fun, and know you deserve it after the work you've done. Keep affirming to yourself that you've done a good job and you deserve good things (fun and relaxation) in your life—because you do!

After your break, set aside some time to sit down with your inventory. Read your lists, slowly, from start to finish, and make notes as you go along. What is really important? What is not that important? Feel free to put stars next to important things and cross off unimportant things. If you've forgotten something important, add it. Take a day or so to identify the most important items and notes on your lists. These should include:

How you feel about losing the positive things
How you feel about losing the negative things

All the things you are angry and hurt about
All the things you will miss about your ex and the relationship
Everything you want to say "thank you" for
Everything you want to say "I'm sorry" for
Any significant statements about the relationship

Once you've identified the most important items on your lists, you'll use this information to write a letter to your ex (that you will not send). Before you begin writing, however, there's one other thing to think about. The last thing that this letter must contain is something most people have trouble with:

Everything you forgive your ex for

When we do this exercise during seminars, there is always pushback from the students. When I say the word *forgive*, people groan. Many have shared the deep hurt they have endured, and forgiveness seems a long way off. One woman shared, "For a long time, I just felt really stuck about the word *forgiveness*. It seemed to be about the other person and I couldn't shake that thinking." But forgiveness is about your own personal moving-on process. It's not a favor you are doing for someone else. It's a favor you are doing for yourself.

When writing the words *I forgive you*, tell yourself this: "*I forgive you* means that I need to begin the process of letting go of what you did to me." Forgiveness is not about the other person, and it doesn't mean that what he or she has done is okay. It simply means, "I know you did this wrong thing, but I need to move on from it because holding onto it is hurting me."

Writing down *I forgive you* is a way to start practicing forgiveness and letting go—even if you don't actually feel it yet. Without forgiveness it's easy to become embroiled and embittered and held down by hatred. You don't have to forgive everything your ex-partner did wrong. There may be some things you can't bring yourself to write down. But write something down, because it is important to start the process.

Once your list is finalized and contains only the important things, it is time to write your letter. Choose which items from the list you really want to mention, and write down all the things you want to say. Write full sentences and do not use bullets or shorthand. Pretend you are having one final conversation with your ex; it might even help to talk aloud as you write.

When you have finished writing your letter, take some time to be by yourself and journal about how you are feeling. Set aside some time in the next few days for a letting-go ritual, described at the end of this chapter.

Resolving Other Relationships

If other significant relationships from your past still affect you today, use the Relationship Inventory to work through every relationship that is still haunting you. Go through them one at a time to discover what in your past still needs to be worked out.

The Life Inventory

> "I dragged my feet on doing the Life Inventory, but once I started writing it, there was so much that came to light. I suddenly was able to see where all the attraction to broken people came from."

"In my family I was the mediator, the one who smoothed things over, who would try to get everyone to calm down. I have always been involved with angry, withholding people and it's been my job to calm them down. I'm sick and tired of it and I want to break free from these debilitating patterns. The Life Inventory has helped me see things clearly and now I can change."

"The 'why' doesn't have to be a mystery. The Life Inventory clears up the mystery. We tend to repeat our history if we don't study it and understand it and then choose to do it differently next time based on what we learn from taking the time to dig deeper."

"The Life Inventory helped me understand a lot of my obsessions when the relationship ended. I suddenly could see not only where they came from but that I could do something about it."

"I wish I had had the good luck to know about combining a Relationship Inventory and a Life Inventory way back when. I did a Relationship Inventory on my own after college, but since I didn't do a Life Inventory, I only knew that somehow [my exes] were a certain type. I knew nothing about codependency. I knew nothing about how one could get stuck to someone who wasn't any good for reasons that were not conscious. When I did both inventories (and I did one right after another), I saw some interesting things about my relationships with my parents and other relatives."

Hopefully your Relationship Inventory helped you to understand your previous relationship and identify the red flags you ignored or missed. However, it's not until you understand how your patterns, unfinished business, and unresolved grief continue to affect you and your choices that you ensure that you will have better relationships.

Many of us have "broken choosers" as the result of our upbringing and past relationships. So we choose people who represent our unfinished business, hoping on a subconscious level to win over that which we have never won. The irony is that we pick people who represent our past struggles, people who are just like those who came before, and in doing so we will never triumph. We need to disengage from people like our former tormentors because the only way to win is not to play the game.

The Life Inventory is a framework for you to finish the business that keeps you reliving your relationship patterns. While the Relationship Inventory teaches you the lessons you need to learn from your last relationship, the Life Inventory teaches you what unhealthy forces are at work and restructures how you relate to other people. The Life Inventory goes back to your childhood and may lead you directly to the Parent (or other caretaker) Inventory before you are even finished with the Life Inventory.

These inventories are designed to show you what is driving you to pick incompatible, unhealthy partners. Once you understand these forces, you can change the way they affect you.

Writing the Life Inventory

1. This first exercise takes, as a starting point, the work you did in the Relationship Inventory. On a blank sheet of paper,

make two columns, one for positive and one for negative. Read over the lists you made about your most recent partner's positive and negative traits. For each trait think about your past partners who had the same or similar traits. If you've had difficult emotional attachments or turbulent relationships of the non-romantic kind, you can include them as well. This can be romantic interests ("crushes"), partners, friends, siblings, cousins, or other peer relationships. In each column, write down which traits of your ex are similar to traits of specific other people in your life.

2. Look over the chart you've made and write down certain similarities and patterns among all or most of the people listed.
3. Make a list of the positive and negative qualities in your mother. How many of your exes or close friends have the same qualities?
4. Make a list of the positive and negative qualities in your father. How many of your exes or close friends have the same qualities?
5. Make a list of the positive and negative qualities of any other significant and influential caretaker or peer. How many of your exes have the same qualities?

As you can see, these lists now allow you to reference and cross-reference all the relationships in your life, past and present. It can take a while to really complete the first five exercises, but even before you are finished, you can move on to the next exercise.

Make another two-column table. On one side write "Negative Traits of People I Am Drawn To," and in that column write a list of the negative qualities that appear consistently in most or all of your significant relationships. On the other side write "Struggle I Am Trying to Win." For example, if most of your exes have been overly critical, you might write "Critical" in the first column. What's the struggle you're trying to win by dating critical people? You may notice that "critical" is also a trait of your father. You may write something like, "Trying to win approval from my critical father." Another possibility is that the critical person wasn't your father but an older sibling whom you adored but who picked on you. If you're unsure about what to write in column two, journal about it, and then come back to it another time.

Your relationships are the most accurate reflection of your emotional health. No relationship can be healthier than its sickest partner. If you look at your partner and your issues with him or her, this will help you to understand who in your past you still have issues with. If you are drawn to people who represent an unhealthy parent, it is probably time to do an inventory about that parent. You may eventually do both parents, but for now it's important to only do one.

The Parent Inventory. Look at the lists you made for your Life Inventory of positive and negative traits for the parent you are focusing on. Think back to your childhood and do the following:

1. Make a list of all the times you wanted this parent to be something he or she was not. Were there times you were disappointed? Embarrassed? Left wanting? Unsure? Were there times you wanted or needed cuddling and this parent was not there? Were there other parents who showed up at

plays or games and yours did not? In what ways was your parent not what you wanted or needed?

2. Make a list of all the negative aspects of your one-on-one relationship. List all the ways this parent treated you, specifically, that were negative. List all the ways that you may have been treated differently than a sibling or all the ways that your personality and your parent's personality simply didn't mesh.
3. Make a list of times you tried to please this parent and failed.
4. Make a list of times you rebelled, and your parent's reaction.
5. Make a list of all the positive aspects of your one-on-one relationship with your parent.
6. Were there times that your relationship worked really well? Were there good times that you remember as special or nice?
7. Make a list of how others in your family interacted with this parent. How did your other parent interact with him or her? How did your siblings interact with him or her? Did you pick up any cues from your other parent about how to respond to this parent's behavior? Did your other parent praise or criticize this parent to you? If so, how did you feel about it?
8. What behaviors did this parent engage in that you tried to change? If you didn't try to change behaviors you disliked, did you think they would change eventually? Did you hope they would change? Were you surprised when this parent acted in a negative way toward you?
9. Did your parent have two extreme personalities? Did you split your parent into good and bad? What were the benefits and consequences of splitting your parent?

10. Write down the things you feel you did wrong as a child in your interactions with your parent. Were there times you were disobedient and disrespectful? Did you lie? Sneak?
11. Write down any significant statements you would have liked to say.
12. Write down all the things you forgive your parent for.

As you did with the Relationship Inventory, finish up the Parent Inventory within a week or two and then take a break and give yourself credit for doing the work. Relax and have fun. Remember, it is always important that you take breaks and reward yourself for doing this work. After a few days, you'll do the same thing with this inventory as you did with your Relationship Inventory. Make a list of the most important things on your Parent Inventory, then write your letter and read it out loud. When you're done, do the letting-go ritual described at the end of the chapter.

As mentioned earlier, you may need to do this inventory about your other parent, older siblings, or other adult caretakers. Go slow and be sure not to rush the work. Between inventories, it's a good idea to use your journal and think about where you'd like to go next. Take breaks between inventories and make sure you are doing them at a healthy pace.

Taking the Relationship and Life Inventories to the Next Level

The truth of relationship healthiness is that water seeks its own level. If you want to know what is missing in you, what unfinished business you have, what your inner struggles are, you need not look further than your partner. If you listen carefully and look closely, usually your choice of mates will tell you what you need to know about yourself. As you grow and change, your choice of mate continues to reflect what you still need to work on.

After you have completed your Relationship Inventory (or inventories) and made progress on your Life Inventory, use the information you have learned as a road map to where you have been and where you don't want to be. Instead of repeating the patterns of the past, it is time to step outside those patterns and take responsibility for yourself and your life.

Chapter 8 looks at new relationships as a reflection of your own emotional health. After doing a few full-blown inventories, you will have in black and white all you need to accurately assess your new relationships. For example, if you do have critical partners in your life, look at the Relationship Inventory for the early warning signs that this could be an issue. Look at new partners through these prisms and don't ignore the early warning signs that a new partner might be hypercritical. This does not mean that you're not ready or didn't work through it, but sometimes it's tough to break an attraction to a certain type. By staying mindful of your inventories, you will be able to break your attraction to the wrong type in the future.

The Letting-Go Ritual

This is a ritual to perform after writing a letter to someone from your past, as described in the Relationship Inventory and the Parent Inventory. Ask a friend or a therapist to listen as you read the letter aloud. Even if you feel self-conscious, it is best to read the letter aloud to someone to validate your process. It should be read slowly so that you can connect with the words on the paper, and make sure that as you read, you are feeling what you are saying. If you need to stop to cry or get angry, do so. Take your time and don't rush through it.

When you are finished reading, talk about how you've felt over the course of doing this exercise, and how you feel now. If you feel angry or sad, just feel the feelings. On the other hand, you might not feel anything at all. Eventually, the numbness will go away and the feelings will return.

Later, burn the letter and say out loud, "Thank you for the time you spent in my life. It is now time for me to let you go with love." Even if you're angry and don't feel love, by saying it this way, your letting go is not angry or spiteful. Letting someone go with love, like forgiveness, is for your own benefit, not the benefit of the other person.

This letting-go ritual is important both emotionally and symbolically. Reading the letter aloud, burning it, and walking away are all very important parts of this ritual. Sometimes the ritual feels cleansing. Other times it brings up more grief. Whatever it does, allow it to happen and know that you are healing.

Doing the letting-go ritual does not mean that it's magically over. It is just one step in your healing process. You might return to the middle phase of grief again, but the pain will lessen over time. If you need to do the letting-go ritual again with a different letter, do it. Just know that every time you do it, you are one step closer to being done.

Other Letting-Go Rituals

Sometimes the letting-go ritual makes you want to get rid of physical representations of the person as well—photographs, letters, rings, gifts, and the like. If you are convinced that now is the time to do this, then do it. If you have any doubt, don't do it. You can put everything in a box and shove it to the back of the closet instead. Later, when you're ready for another cleansing ritual, you can get rid of some or all of these items.

Some people prefer to get rid of all reminders of the other person at once, while for others it's preferable to let go more gradually. Do it at your own speed, and don't assume that you need to be completely over your grief all at once or that the letting-go ritual is the final step in getting over it. Sometimes it is. Other times it's just one stage in the letting-go process. Be gentle with yourself if you need to have more than one letting-go ritual.

A Final Word on Forgiveness

As you go through your inventories about your relationships and your primary caretakers, you'll find yourself in different phases of emotions as well as different phases of forgiveness. Final and full forgiveness is very freeing, but it's a process and not a one-time thing. And it's only freeing when it is done at the right time for the right reason.

If you refuse to forgive, you run the risk of becoming bitter and unable to let go. If you rush to forgiveness, you may never confront the anger and pain you sometimes feel for this person who hurt you. If you forgive too soon, you may find yourself open to being hurt again, perhaps even by the same person. If you take too long to forgive, you become unable to love others.

Forgiveness, like grief and like the inventories, is done in phases. When you are writing your inventories and going through your grieving process, you might find yourself seething with anger, melting with hatred, and cursing the existence of someone who hurt you. This doesn't feel great. However, although it is not healthy to act on them, these feelings are temporary and normal and natural. You should acknowledge these feelings, work through them, process them, and later let them go.

At the beginning of your breakup, you might have been told by others to let go of your anger and forgive, that you'll feel so much better. The truth is that you can only forgive after you've worked through your anger and pain. Working through the inventories in this chapter and writing the letters are the first steps to forgiveness. In the letting-go ritual, you read your letter out loud and it included the phrase *I forgive you for . . .* That might not have been entirely true—you may not have completely forgiven. And that is okay.

Sometimes you can forgive only a percentage, and the remaining percentage is what it is. You learn to live with it. You may go back later and find your percentages have changed. The bottom line is that forgiveness rarely happens all at once. Instead, forgiveness is the end of a long process, and it comes when it comes. Sometimes you have to decide to forgive, even though it's hard, because you know it's time. Other times you try but you know it's not time yet. The important thing is to do it after you've spent the time you need being hurt and angry, and after you've said (to your journal, therapist, sponsor, or friends) all the nasty things you want to say about the person who hurt you.

Forgiveness is part of the healing process. Don't ignore it, but don't rush to it either. It will happen when it happens. And when it does, it will be a benefit to you. You will feel the cleansing power of forgiveness and move on even more. Forgive in time, when you are ready, and after you've allowed yourself to feel your strongest emotions. Then forgive with all your might, and be okay with yourself.

The inventories described in this chapter are where you get to step back, look at everything in your life, and work on what needs to change. As time goes on, these inventories can be done over again and developed to fit your changing needs. Once you know what really happened in your past relationships, and where you really are in your life, you can begin to heal the past. You can fully grieve your unresolved grief, finish your unfinished business, and move forward.

7

Where Do You End and I Begin? Developing Limits and Boundaries

"I am really excited about setting some clear, unmistakable, don't-even-go-there boundaries. There have been some small victories already and I'm learning to spot when people start to push at the fence to see if it will fall over."

"No one listened to me because I backed down on what I wanted every single time. I was miserable and felt victimized. Once I started setting boundaries, things changed."

"Setting boundaries was the single most loving thing I've done for myself in my entire life. It changed the game completely. Now I'm winning."

"People didn't like when I first started setting boundaries, but I figured it was better that I like me than that they do. Before I got boundaries, I did not like me very much."

> "Changing my boundaries with my parents has had the greatest (most positive) impact on my life overall. From there, it's gotten so much easier to have good boundaries with everyone else. The second-greatest impact has been on my kids. I've been beating myself [up] for years for not being a good enough mom, and that has really been coming to an end. No drama, no big scene, no guilt—just a 'no' in response to certain things when that is the simple answer that is needed with both parents and children."

> "I finally realized that no one can crash my boundaries without my permission. This 'small' revelation has changed my life."

Do you feel like people tend to walk all over you? Do you have a hard time saying no? Are you afraid to express your needs to a partner for fear of an argument or of being left? Do you feel "mean" if you don't let someone do what he or she wants? Are you afraid people won't like you if you tell them that something they're doing is not okay with you?

Previous chapters have talked about setting boundaries with children and ex-partners, but it's important to develop boundaries with everyone in your life. This is because strong boundaries result in good relationships, high self-esteem, and emotional well-being. People who set proper limits enjoy successful lives because it's easier to take chances and risks when you know you can protect yourself. But putting them into place in your life is a hard task. It won't happen overnight, and it's not necessarily going to be easy, but it makes life much simpler in the long run.

What Are Boundaries?

Quite simply, boundaries are a border, a limit, or a standard. To apply this to human relationships, codependency expert Melody Beattie says that a boundary is simply the recognition that you begin and end someplace, and I begin and end someplace else. This means what's yours is yours and what's mine is mine, and we are clear on the difference. I am responsible for my thoughts, feelings, and actions, and you are responsible for yours. I am responsible for how much I allow others to put on me or take from me. Having boundaries also means that

> you know which problems, responsibilities, obligations, and jobs belong to others and which belong to you, and, therefore, you don't have unproductive and endless arguments about them;
>
> you know how to say no, and when you say yes it's of your own volition and without coercion, feelings of guilt, or an overblown sense of duty;
>
> you set limits on how much you give to others and know the supply is not endless;
>
> you have clearly defined limits with parents, children, friends, lovers, work acquaintances, storekeepers, customer-service representatives, the bank teller, the reservation clerk, the cat sitter, the dog groomer—everyone—and no one takes advantage of you;
>
> you take care of yourself and let people know that they can't invade the space you have defined as yours;

you say what you mean and mean what you say, without being mean; and

your needs get met because you are not afraid to say what they are.

Why Set Boundaries?

Because boundary setting can be difficult, people often wonder if it's worth it. It is. As you observe people, you will find that some people are "boundary crashers"—controlling people who have no sense of personal limits and ownership. People with good boundaries cannot be controlled by these crashers because they don't allow themselves to be. But people without boundaries or with very weak ones usually have a wealth of controllers and users in their lives. The goal is to have healthier relationships with healthier people. Therefore, boundary setting is a must.

Setting clear boundaries will enable you to not fear interaction with others. When you know you are able to protect yourself no matter what, you are better able to let down your guard when the time is right, and truly love and be loved by others. Ironically, having clearly defined borders, limits, and standards leads to true intimacy and sharing.

When to Set a Boundary

A healthy life starts with knowing when to set a boundary—being able to express your opinion or indicate to another person that his or her behavior is not acceptable to you. If you're journaling and observing yourself in different situations, pay attention to the times you get upset. Write down what is going on between you and the other person, and try to figure out whether these frustrating exchanges are clues that you need to set a boundary. Listen carefully to how people treat you and compare this to how you want to be treated. Journal about these times and think about what you can say or do differently. Later in this chapter you'll find some examples of how people deal with boundaries, which will help you to find ways to set them in your own life. The first step, though, is merely to identify *when* you may need to set a boundary.

The first signal that you need a boundary is feeling hurt, frustrated, angry, or put upon. If someone berates you for not doing something that is not your responsibility, you might feel defensive and hurt but not know how to say, "This is not my responsibility." If someone crashes your boundary by dumping information on you that you don't want, you might feel distressed but not know how to say, "I really don't want to hear about that." If someone borrows something and doesn't return it or doesn't return it in good condition, you might feel angry but not know how to say, "I would appreciate it if you return my things in the condition in which I gave them to you." If someone continually asks you to bail him or her out, you might feel exasperated but not know how to say, "I'm sorry but I can't help you this time."

If you ask someone to close the window because you feel cold and he or she says, "You can't be cold," you may not realize that this person is crashing your boundaries. If you're angry and someone says, "That's nothing to be angry over," you may question your feelings rather than question this person's right to comment on your feelings. You may not know enough to say, "My feelings are not right or wrong. They just are." But any time someone invalidates your feelings, whether physical or emotional, you need to let him or her know that you do not appreciate being told how you feel.

Any time you feel upset by someone, chances are you need to set a boundary. Your pattern may be that it is easier for you to sit with your own upset than to hurt someone else's feelings. But if you're going to have good boundaries, you have to start recognizing that your feelings are valid and crashers have to stop imposing on you. Learning to set and enforce boundaries can be tough at first, but it's worth the work. Using many of the tools you're already working with, you can learn to set boundaries, and eliminate the negative feelings you're having about your interactions or the people you're interacting with.

How to Set Boundaries

1. Observation. The first step toward establishing healthy boundaries with those around you is to journal about the situations that crop up where you feel put upon, frustrated, hurt, angry, taken advantage of, or not respected.
2. Recognize that boundary setting takes time because it is both a skill and a state of mind. You don't wake up one day and say, "I'm going to set boundaries with the entire world in every situation I ever come to." That's not going to work. You'll set all the boundaries you need over time, but be patient and go about it a little bit at a time.

3. Limit the "chances" that others get to crash your boundaries. A woman once said to me, "I find it hard not to give people chances. Not everyone responds the first time because they either didn't hear you or didn't understand." This is true; setting boundaries often involves simply repeating your position, but do not repeat your position more than three times. Boundary crashers want to wear you out, and wear you down, and will pretend not to hear even when they do. If you've made the same statement three times, they have heard it, and it's time to stop "trying" to be heard and set a boundary.
4. Always use "I" language. When you deliver boundaries in "I" language, it helps to keep the other person from becoming defensive. Even if he or she argues with you, the response is, "I'm simply saying this is how I feel," and how you feel needs to be okay in any relationship.
5. When setting boundaries, it's best to keep the conversation short and sweet. People always ask me what to say when they are asked to explain. Too often people with no boundaries have gotten into the habit of overexplaining themselves or thinking that they must clarify their position and make someone understand. That is not true; you don't need to explain anything to anyone if you don't want to. A coaching client of mine decided, after spending a vacation with a boundary crasher, that she had had enough of being with this person who disrespected her, invalidated her feelings, and told her what to do. So tired of it was she that she decided she was not going to the boundary crasher's next event. She asked me, "Do I tell her a white lie?" I said, "No, just tell her you're not going." She said, "What if she wants

an explanation?" I said unless you want to get into a long, drawn-out argument with someone who does not respect your thoughts and feelings, you need to simply say, "I'm sorry, I'm unable to attend," and leave it at that.

6. Know that you're going to be uncomfortable, rattled even, when others press for an explanation. A blog reader accurately described the almost universal experience of starting to set boundaries:

   It's not about setting boundaries, but finding the correct script by which to deliver them. After being a mush for so long, I tend to get uneasy delivering the bad news. Sometimes I don't speak as confidently as I'd like. I don't want things to degenerate (or escalate) into a fight. I feel clunky, like a bull in a china shop. I figure it'll get better as I get some more experience standing up for myself, but in the meantime, I feel like I'm a jerk sometimes.

   You are going to feel like a "jerk" sometimes. Your initial efforts may be "clunky" and sometimes you will lose the fight to keep explanations out of it; but it's important to keep trying. Affirm your right to set good boundaries without detailed explanations.

7. Preparation: Choose your battles wisely. Think about where you need to set boundaries the most, and focus on these areas for now. Pick two or three places to start, and know why you are choosing these areas. What are the most pressing boundary issues in your life? Journal possible scenarios and outcomes as you set boundaries.

8. Never announce a boundary, give an ultimatum, or state a consequence unless you can follow through. The point of setting boundaries is to let people know where you begin and end and where they begin and end. If you're unclear about that, then others will be unclear about it, too. It won't change a thing in your life if you set a boundary that you cannot follow through with.
9. Don't worry about hurt feelings. Beattie writes that you cannot simultaneously set a boundary and take care of someone else's feelings. So know that it's either boundary setting or caring for someone else. Sit with the discomfort that someone is angry with you, because it means you are taking care of yourself. If it's not okay with the other person, it has to be okay with you. Journal about your feelings, but affirm that you are entitled to your boundaries.

Before embarking on boundary setting with a particular individual, know that preparation is key. For example, let's say your mother always calls you on Friday to ask you to run errands on Saturday and this upsets you. It's been this way for a long time, even though you've been frustrated with it since the beginning. In the past, you've tried to extract yourself from the obligation by making excuses, maybe even lying to her a few times, but you've always been afraid to say no.

Write in your journal how you will set a boundary with your mother. You might say, "I'm sorry, but I cannot pick you up on Saturday." Now imagine her many responses. She might say, "After all I've done for you! You can't even pick me up on Saturday." And imagine yourself saying, "I'm sorry, Mom, but I can't do it this week." Write down everything your mother has done in the past to "guilt-trip" you and manipulate you. Write down all the things she could say to you and what your answer would be. Practice it. Go over it in your head. Visualize it. Affirm to yourself that you set boundaries with your mother. Affirm that it's okay to say no to your mother.

Maybe in the past your mother has questioned you, sometimes relentlessly, about what you're doing instead of taking her on errands. Don't get sucked in this time. Don't feel that you need to explain yourself to her—in fact, don't explain yourself to her. Write this down so you stop before you get trapped into explaining. Just say, "I'm sorry, Mom, I can't pick you up to run errands this week." She might say, "You haven't answered my question." And you can say, "I'm not answering the question. I said I was sorry that I can't run errands this week." She may try to make it about your not answering the question, she may try to bargain with you, to get you to do it earlier or later or on Sunday. This is what boundary crashers do when you are new at setting boundaries and they are trying to go up, over, and around the boundary. Step back and observe how crazily a crasher can behave when you set a boundary and they don't like it. Listen for the manipulation and the scare tactics. It will amaze you when you listen for it.

A woman in Al-Anon once told me, "When we stop people pleasing, people are not pleased." It's true. They are not pleased and they will do everything to reverse your resolve. Do not give in. Do not allow bargaining. Shut down the conversation if you need to. Keep reminding yourself: The goal is not answering the questions and not giving in.

It's not necessary to make others understand your actions, and it can be hard to say no without adding an explanation. However, there are many times when you need to be firm and say nothing more. If you start to explain, you may find yourself arguing and trying to defend your position and eventually crumble and give in. It's better to just say no. It takes practice to do this, especially if you've been explaining yourself (usually to no avail) for a long time. People will wait for an explanation or push for one. Don't give it. It will be uncomfortable, but let it be. In time it will get easier.

Natural and Logical Consequences

Other times, setting boundaries is more complicated than just saying no. We need to "enforce" the boundary with consequences to those who don't respect it. As I discussed in Chapter 5, boundary setting with children involves allowing natural consequences and giving logical consequences. These consequences can also be applied to adults. No one is ever going to respect a boundary you've set if there is no consequence for not respecting it.

Natural Consequences. First of all think about the question, who owns this problem when loved ones get into legal or financial trouble? There is a saying, "A failure to plan on your part does not constitute an emergency on mine." This means, do not allow others to make their problems yours. Yes, it is hard to say no, but if you bail people out time and again, they never learn from the natural consequences that flow from their actions or inactions. By not allowing those we love the dignity of standing on their own two feet, we continue to control them and keep them in our debt. It's time to stop bailing them out, stop rescuing, and stop taking on responsibility that is not yours. It's hard to let go of the reins and sit with the discomfort that something bad will befall someone you love, but that is exactly what you need to do. Not only will your life be better, but your loved one will learn something everyone needs to know: self-responsibility.

Again, think about different areas in your life where you need to set limits, or scenarios that seem to come up all the time. Is it a person asking you for money? Is it someone pushing his or her responsibility on you? What is it in your life that needs changing the most?

Next, plan out the scenario in your journal, like a game of chess: Write down what moves the boundary crasher will make, and how you will respond. If the boundary crasher says or does X, I will say Y. If the boundary crasher does not respond, I need to allow the natural consequence to occur or relay the following logical consequence.

It's always hard to foresee what a crasher will do when you set a boundary, and he or she may well do something that even your most diligent preparation has not equipped you for. But as you become more observant and in tune with boundary crashing, you can sketch out various ways to deal with these unpredictable reactions. Practice saying no and practice shutting down the argument in your head or role-play with your therapist or friends. You can prepare for boundary crashers and their drama.

Logical Consequences. While it's hard to allow natural consequences to run their course, it can be harder to figure out and enforce a logical consequence. Here's an example from a student of mine, Jenna, who had a friend, Marie, who always showed up late when they had plans to go somewhere together. Marie's behavior would cause them to miss the beginning of movies or dinner reservations or be late for important engagements. These times upset Jenna but didn't seem to faze Marie. Jenna tried chiding Marie, tried to make her feel guilty, tried countless reminders and even got angry a few times. But nothing changed because there was no consequence for Marie's behavior. Jenna told me, "I always wait for her and she constantly ruins my night."

I told her that Marie did nothing of the kind. In fact, Jenna ruined her own night by giving Marie that much power and not setting any boundaries through the years. Jenna complained that she had no idea how to set a boundary, since she had tried everything except going on ahead without Marie. But going ahead without her *is* the solution. Jenna needed to set a boundary and then give logical consequences in response to Marie's behavior.

I told Jenna to explain to Marie—remember, using "I" language—how she feels and that she can't tolerate being late for everything any longer. Tell Marie simply that she will go on without her if she's not there on time. She told Marie, "When I am expecting you and you're not here, I feel as if I need to cancel the rest of my plans and wait for you, and that upsets me. I'd love for us to go together, but I feel resentful when I just wait for you, so I think it would be a good idea if I just went on ahead if you're not here by the time we've agreed to meet."

I had told Jenna to be prepared for backlash and protest. As a GPYP blog reader pointed out, "[When you set boundaries,] be prepared to be told off, belittled, berated, sometimes by people you've known for years, [people you] can't believe are saying [these things]. But know that you are becoming the person you were meant to be, and it's their loss for not welcoming or appreciating the transformation." It's important to stand your ground when met with resistance to your new boundaries, even when it's tough.

If Marie had a problem with Jenna's new boundary, she might push back on her or argue the point. I advised Jenna not to explain or justify, but simply reiterate the boundary and her plan to go on ahead. Repeat, in a calm manner, "Well, I'd love to go with you. Please be on time or I'll have to go ahead." Jenna has given Marie two choices and only two choices: Show up on time, or I'll go on ahead. I predicted that her friend, like most people, might challenge her, and that is exactly what happened.

They made plans to meet at Jenna's house and drive together to a mutual friend's party. At the appointed meeting time, Marie was nowhere to be found, so Jenna went out to her car. Just as she was leaving, her cell phone rang. "I'm almost there. Wait for me," Marie said. Jenna was frozen for a minute but knew that her boundary was still being crossed, so she told Marie she was going on without her and would meet her there. Marie, who had taken advantage of her for years, could not believe Jenna was being so "unreasonable."

Jenna reiterated her boundary in a friendly tone. "Marie, I said I was leaving at seven o'clock if you weren't here, and you aren't here. It's okay. I will meet you there." And she hung up. Had Jenna not done the hard, uncomfortable work of setting this boundary, Marie would have found the "hole" in the boundary, and each week the hole would have gotten bigger. By being firm on her boundary and the consequences for not respecting the boundary, Jenna has done the hard work once, and it will pay off in the future. Giving in to the discomfort now would just result in more frustration for her later.

It's Okay to Set Boundaries

Remember that it's difficult the first few times you set boundaries with any given person in any given area, but it will get easier. Walk through the boundary and the consequences you will enforce if people challenge you—and people will challenge you the first time or even the first few times. Allow yourself to be uncomfortable with it. Sometimes you'll have to face a very tough situation where you know that you have to set a boundary, and it's going to be a universally unpopular decision. Stay strong. You can do it. People will respect you, and over time there will be less and less haggling or melodrama. Eventually it will become less necessary to even set these boundaries. Eventually people will know you mean it when you say, "Please be on time."

Remember that it's okay to have desires, opinions, limits, and personal space. It's also okay not to tell people everything, not to explain everything, not to be available sometimes, and for people not to have any idea where you are. One of my mentors told me a long time ago that a ringing phone is a request, not a demand. I see too many people allowing their family and friends to interrupt them wherever and whenever thanks to cell phones and computers. Or if someone calls them and they don't answer, the person will later say, "Why didn't you answer your cell phone?" That's a question you only have to answer if people have trained you to think that you must answer your phone at all times.

It's okay not to answer a phone, and it's okay not to lend money, books, or clothing. Really—it's okay not to do any of these things. If it's an emergency, he will get in touch with you. If she really needs the book, she will go to the library. If he really needs the money, he'll talk to someone else. It's okay that you're not there for everything and everyone. People will respect you for that. How long have you been answering your cell phone every time it rings? And how many of those calls have been emergencies? It's okay not to answer your phone. It's okay not to be available by phone, by IM, by e-mail, or by voice mail. You deserve your privacy and "off" time. Respect that about yourself, and others will too. Remember that boundary setting is not about upsetting someone else, it's about taking care of yourself.

Who Owns What?

We've mentioned a few times now that it's important when setting boundaries to know who owns what. An illustration of this might be a neighbor who asks you to take his mother to the doctor because he knows your day off is on Wednesday. It seems to happen time and time again that his mother has a doctor's appointment on your day off. You've taken her a few times, but you would like not to have to take her again. You have other things to do on Wednesdays, and even when you don't, you would like to have a chance to relax.

Let's think about who owns this problem. Whose mother is this? Not yours. Whose doctor's appointment is it? Not yours. Do you own this problem? No. The next step is to say, "I would if I could, but I have other things to do." Try to leave it at that. Unfortunately, you might have caved in before, or your neighbor might sense that you will cave this time, so he will push. Remember, you will be challenged when you first set a boundary. Just reiterate what you've said already. If you have to say it a third time, fine, but that is it. After three times you can say, "I'd love to talk to you more, but I have to go now." Then go. Do not allow him to pull you back.

This is a very obvious example of ownership. But many times ownership is less clear. Let's take, for example, the newly separated couple John and Laura. When they were still together, they visited his grandmother, who lives an hour away, every week so she could see their children. Since they've been separated, the children have not seen Great-Grandma. Although Laura is not working right now, she's overwhelmed with the separation and doesn't really want to spend time with the soon-to-be-former in-laws. John is very angry when he calls Laura and says, "Why haven't you taken the kids to see Grandma?" Laura instinctively wants to apologize or to take the kids to see Grandma, but let's think about this.

Whose grandma is she?

Yes, she's his grandma, but Laura's loyalty to the woman goes back many years. Still, Grandma has complained to her grandson and not to Laura. And the bottom line is she's John's grandmother, not Laura's.

Even if there are shades of gray, even if there are nuances to consider, break the situation down to the most basic form and make it black and white. Spending too much time in the gray areas confuses a situation. Yes, Laura had a relationship with John's grandmother, and yes, there is some sort of loyalty there, but the bottom line is she's John's grandmother.

Whose kids are they?

Again, this is a bit of a gray area because, of course, they are both John's and Laura's kids. In this instance, though, his grandmother wants to see them because they're John's kids and not because they're Laura's.

Who owns the problem of getting the kids to Grandma?

John.

Laura must let John know she does not own this problem. She can say, "I will be happy to have you come over and pick up the kids to visit your grandmother. Just let me know when." If John continues to chastise her or berate her or try to invoke the gray areas, she needs to sidestep his comments. Otherwise she will get lost in an argument. Laura needs to repeat, "I will be happy to have you come over and pick up the kids to visit your grandmother. Just let me know when." On the third time she repeats herself she should say, "Let me know when. I have to go now. Goodbye." Then she must hang up the phone and not pick it up if he calls back. This is his problem. He needs to own it.

Boundary-Setting Review

1. Remember, *no* is a one-word sentence. If you don't want to do something for someone, say no and move on. Do not allow someone to demand an explanation or cajole or manipulate you. No is no. It's not yes, and do not allow it to

become yes. If you allow a no to become a yes, your no will never mean the same thing again.

2. Do not ask for something or repeat your boundary more than three times. The answer is no, and it's not changing to yes. If a person doesn't get this after you've said it three times, he or she is not ever going to, so just end the conversation.
3. Allow others to suffer natural consequences of their actions.
4. Give logical consequences for not respecting your boundaries.
5. Allow others to be angry. You're setting limits that haven't been there before. So the other person might push back, might tell you that you're unreasonable, might bring up other issues that are irrelevant to the current conversation.
6. Do not allow people to pull you into other things that have nothing to do with what's going on at the moment. Don't get into a big shouting match. Don't talk about other situations. Don't defend against "laundry lists" (things you've done wrong since the beginning of time).
7. Use your affirmations to help you enforce your boundaries. Write affirmations such as "I have clear boundaries in my life" or "I set clear boundaries with others."
8. Use "I" statements to take blame and defensiveness out of your communications. Practice "I" statements in your journal. Write them down and say them out loud. These "I" statements let people know how you feel and what you want them to stop doing.

"I feel upset when you call me at the last minute to change plans with me."

"I feel angry when you call me in the middle of the day and get upset when I can't talk because I'm at work."

"I feel judged when you come into my house and ask if something happened because the house isn't clean."

"I feel judged when you question my child-rearing decisions."

9. Remember it's okay not to tell people everything, not to explain everything, and to say no. It's okay to set boundaries. In fact, it's necessary for a happy and healthy life.

Setting boundaries takes practice, but after a while having good, healthy ones will make your life easier. Relationships and friendships will be easier. Put the work in up front, and you will reap many, many rewards.

8

Moving On: The Path to Real Love

"Working through the grief after my last breakup changed my life. I would never tolerate constant competition for a partner's attention again—I know I am worth being number one now and will not settle for less. My partner gets the same from me."

"Every day that you honor yourself and what you know in your heart and mind to be true, you take another step toward being a person who will be honored by others."

"After my last relationship ended, I realized that I was only in a relationship because I thought people would think I was a loser if I wasn't. Now that I'm doing what I want and building my own life, I realize I would like to spend some time—years, maybe—getting to know me. And it doesn't matter what anyone else thinks about that."

"I used to look at dating as something I had to do to get to a relationship. Now I'm just thinking of it as a learning experience."

"I have a large, pretty opinionated family, but I knew I had made progress when I stopped evaluating the women that I dated through the eyes of my family. Now I just go and meet them and leave the rest of the family home and out of my head."

"[In] the next relationship (if there is one), I will ONLY settle for being number one, first place, and a prize. I have my flaws and issues and I'm working on [them,] so I won't ever accept the 'I'm confused' mind-set again. My answer to that nowadays would be, 'That's too bad, because I'm not, goodbye.' End of story."

All the work you've been doing since your breakup is making you a better, stronger, and healthier person. You've been getting to know who you are and figuring out what you want, where you'd like to go in life, and how to get there. Some people may be surprised to find that once they get used to being alone, it's really quite nice and they'd like to stay single for a while. At some point, though, you'll probably start to think about dating or being in a relationship again. The questions that most people ask when thinking about this time are, "How do I know when I'm ready to date?" "How do I know when I'm ready to be in a relationship?" "How do I know if I really like being alone or I'm just too scared to go out and try again?" "How do I deal with others who think I should be doing something else?"

Whether you're ready to consider dating again, or you're still figuring out if you're enjoying your life or just hiding out, all the work you've done so far will help you answer these questions. This chapter should provide you with some ways to look at the work you've done in order to find more answers.

Loving Again or Living Alone

You should have a lot of material to review as you plan ahead: your journal, your inventories, your goal worksheets, and various other task lists and guides. Ideally you've been keeping a log of where you are, where you've been, and where you're going. This information will be valuable to you when you're ready to evaluate your readiness for a new relationship.

Being Single

Even if your goal is to be part of a couple again someday, it's important to discover that being single is an acceptable way of life—whether you're living alone or with family and friends. Before becoming part of a functional couple, you must learn to be functional solo and know that being alone is not a punishment or an adverse way of life. Being healthy means recognizing the joys and benefits of being alone, and that forging your life on your own is something to be proud of.

The first challenge is ignoring what others may think or say about your singlehood. Other people may put a lot of pressure on you to be part of a couple, assuming that being in a relationship is what you want. You may even feel that pressure from society in general. To assess what's best for you, it's important to resist the opinions of others who think you should "get back in the game" or find "The One" as soon as possible. No matter what your friends, family, mainstream media, or popular culture tells you, being part of a couple does not necessarily mean being happy.

In fact, statistics seem to suggest the opposite. The sad truth is that half of all first marriages and more than half of all second marriages end in divorce, and breakup rates are even higher for nonmarital relationships. And of those who do stay together for many years, a large number stay together out of codependency or out of denial about how miserable they really are. Others stay in bad relationships out of fear of the unknown or fear of being alone. So it is safe to say that coupledom is not always bliss, and "happily ever after" is not always that happy, even in the cases where it is "ever after."

But that's not to say that you can't beat the odds. To be happy with someone else, it's important to be happy alone. One of the reasons you've invested so much time and effort into building your own life is that being a strong and healthy person attracts similar people, both friends and lovers. On the flip side, if you can't stand the aloneness or think you have to be in a relationship to be socially accepted, you are always going to settle for less. If you can't be by yourself, you will attract others who can't be alone, and your relationships will be formed out of unhealthy dependency. One important benefit of learning to be alone is that it allows you to choose whom to have in your life—friends, lovers, acquaintances, family members—and to choose these people from a position of strength.

Last year I was teaching a seminar and talked about the benefits of spending some time alone, after the grief has ended and things are looking up. One of my students came to me during the break and said, "But I can't stand the deadly silence, the loneliness, and the boredom." Remember your positive attitude and self-talk. If you assess aloneness as *deadly silence* instead of as *empowering quietude*, then it will always be hard to be alone. Think of the peace as the sound of your own life working. Write some affirmations about the positive aspects of being alone.

Learning to be alone is a freedom unlike any other. It means you can be okay by yourself and, therefore, will not tether yourself to someone who doesn't treat you well. Learning to be alone means that if you do enter a relationship, you know that you will be okay no matter what. Knowing that you are able to handle life alone gives you self-respect, and that self-respect becomes a demand that others treat you accordingly.

What it comes down to is this: You can't find the right person for you if you're not right with yourself. Self-acceptance begins with the work you've been doing since Chapter 4—finding out what you enjoy, cultivating your hobbies and interests, indulging in self-pampering, and making new friends. Being alone means not being afraid of times when you do feel lonely. Healthy people learn how to sit with times of loneliness and don't try to avoid them. Healthy people are okay with being bored, restless, and uncomfortable without having to assuage these feelings immediately. Learn to just go with the flow. Be okay with the silence. Make peace with the peace.

Whether you decide to be alone for a while as a stopover on the way to exploring the world of dating and relationships, or you've decided that you want to spend several years living single, do learn to build your own space and thrive in it. Having your own life will give you a feeling of security that nothing else can, and will make all of your future relationships and endeavors that much better. You will develop a solid attitude that you can take care of you and yours.

And good, healthy people are attracted to that attitude. One of my students told me that when she took the time to be by herself and build her own life, a remarkable thing happened. Her life actually filled up with more interests and more people. She said,

> The paradox of being able to be alone and live your own life is that you meet so many others who are able to do the same, and your life becomes bountiful. You meet people and go places and life is just so enjoyable. When I want to take a break, I read or tend to my home. I've made peace with the peace and have lots of new friends to enjoy. It's the best of both worlds.

By making peace with yourself, you will attract those who like independent people with full, rich lives—whether friendships, work relationships, or romantic relationships. And instead of being alone, you will have more friends and more activities than you ever dreamed possible. Take some time to build your life and it will fill with amazing things.

Dating

When you reach the point where your life is starting to work and, for the most part, you're feeling okay, it might be time to think about dating again. It's important to approach dating with a positive, relaxed attitude—after all, it's going to be hard if you think of it as either evaluating and being evaluated, or nothing more than the precursor to a relationship.

Dating gives you opportunities to practice your observation skills. Think of dating as learning to be comfortable with new people and possible romantic interests, and this will help keep the pressure off. If you're not worrying about being judged or trying to decide whether you could buy a house in the suburbs with this person, you'll be a lot more relaxed, which will make the experience more enjoyable for both of you.

Dating will also give you more information about yourself. By observing yourself during your interactions with potential romantic partners, you'll gather information for your ongoing self-assessment, which will tell you how far you've come and will help you gauge what work you still need to do. Remember, regardless of how any of your dates turn out, you are learning to observe; you are learning to just be you and be okay with that.

The Fifteen Not-So-Simple Rules of Healthy Dating.

1. Enjoy yourself. Dating need not be a chore or a thing you must "go through" between relationships. Think of it as an opportunity to go new places and meet new people. If you don't continue seeing someone romantically, you may develop a friendship or a networking opportunity.
2. Stay safe. Keep first dates casual, doing things such as going to lunch or getting coffee. This allows you to keep the outing short and informal. Meet in public places where there are other people around. Safety is more important than being polite. If you start to think this person is bad news, trust your intuition and bail early. Just excuse yourself and go (or don't excuse yourself, just slip out a side door). Similarly,

don't give new people your home phone number or address. This advice is not meant to scare you, but to remind you to be safe.

3. When you go out, sit back and relax. If you're normally chatty, try to hold off and listen to the other person. If you're normally shy and reserved, try to take more initiative in the conversation. Keep the conversation light and breezy. Do not reveal deep, dark secrets, and do not talk about your ex—even if your date is talking about his or her ex. Do not trade war stories. If your date specifically asks you to tell him or her about your former relationship, give a blithe response. It's a good idea to have a sound bite ready in case the question comes up. You might say, "We wanted different things." If your date continues to press for information, say you really don't want to spend your date talking about your ex. Take note of how your date responds when you push back.
4. Learn to listen to what others are actually saying, not what you hope they are saying. Be aware of the spin machine in your head. ("Oh, you like chocolate ice cream? I like chocolate ice cream too!") Also listen for your date's tendency to broad-stroke all possible compatibilities. Is either of you trying to twist everything into proof of compatibility? It's important to have significant things in common, but liking the same soft drinks doesn't count.
5. Don't reveal too much of yourself on early dates. Sit back and think about whether you like this person, not whether this person likes you. Let go of self-consciousness and stop wondering what he or she is thinking. The most important

thing to decide on early dates is what you think of him or her. Reveal skeletons in your closet or other important information at the right moment. If you have something you'd want someone who will be involved with you to know, it's okay to tell him or her, in a matter-of-fact way, three or four dates down the line. You don't have to come out with this information on a first date—and, in fact, you shouldn't. Your personal information is precious. Guard it and share it slowly. But if you do have something important to tell a potential partner, don't wait until it feels like you're being dishonest by not saying it.

6. Avoid long conversations in the days following the date. You need time to think and to assess this person. Don't get sucked into regular e-mailing, texting, or talking on the phone with someone you have met only once or twice. Take it slow and don't be available for endless conversation.
7. Do not get intensely physical on the first few dates. Being too physical too fast will distort your view of what is really going on. Physical compatibility is much more common than mental or emotional compatibility. Don't misread physical sparks for real compatibility.
8. After each date, journal about your reactions and responses. Have you changed since your last relationship? What insight did you get that was different than you thought it would be? What work do you still need to do on yourself? Journal about any early warning signs you notice in the person. If there are early warning signs, end it. Don't try to justify or explain away the warning signs, just get out. Look at the people you are dating to gather clues about your own

progress. Even if these people are not "relationship material," if they are pleasant enough people you may still want to spend some time with them. A blog reader wrote that it concerned him that all of the women he seemed to be dating were recently separated. He had been to a GPYP seminar and believed me when I said, "Water seeks its own level." He was concerned that none of these women seemed like they were relationship-ready. He asked, "Is their marital status a reflection of where I am right now?" I said I believed it was, but that didn't mean it was a bad thing. If you're attracting and attractive to people who are, for some reason, not ready to be in a serious relationship but seem to be decent and honest people, have fun with it. Go out and have a good time. It's part of the process. This doesn't mean you should engage in a series of one-night stands or shallow flirtations, but recognize that you're not ready and they're not ready, but you can still be respectful and enjoy each other's company without making a big deal about it.

9. If you *are* both interested, go slowly. Allow yourself to have several real dates—where you meet, go out somewhere, and go home separately—before making any decisions about where this is headed. Don't sleep together, don't move in, don't lend money, and don't start a relationship. Before jumping in, figure out if this is what you want, and figure out if this is leading where you think it's leading.
10. Don't allow yourself to be pushed too fast. If the other person has issues with your going slow, then you can say, "I need to take things slowly. If this is too slow for you, please let me know and we can stop seeing each other." You don't

want to be in a relationship with someone who is going to be pushy or possessive. You want someone who respects your boundaries. The minute someone pushes you before you are ready, it's time for the big NEXT! sign to come down.

11. When you're not feeling anyone and no one is feeling you, it's easy to think it will be this way forever. But this is not true, and not a productive way of thinking. Don't get depressed over prospects, and don't take it personally. Perhaps you're not ready to date, and others are picking up that you're not ready. Or perhaps you're still picking the wrong type. Rethink your usual type, since your type seems to be breaking your heart.
12. Stay out of the future. If a date goes badly, don't latch on to the feeling that you will be alone for the rest of your life. If it goes well, don't start picking out tuxedos and china patterns. It's not necessarily the start of the rest of your life. If it goes badly, it's not the end of the world. Just take it, either way, as a day in your life. It was just a date. Leave it at that. Take everything as it comes. Once you take the desperation out of dating—and that includes the desperation to have a great time or find the perfect mate—you will do better with it. You will be less attached to the outcome and more involved in the evaluation of each person and what your reaction to the person is telling you.
13. Accept rejection without self-judgment. If you strike up a cyber conversation and the person cuts it off after seeing your photograph, don't take it personally. It does not mean that you are not attractive, it's that he or she is looking for a certain type and you're not it. If your date does not want

to see you again, don't think there is anything wrong with you. The only way to be successful at dating is to do it without expectations and without taking anything personally. Dating is not about being accepted or rejected. It's about finding the right match.

14. No matter what happens, don't see one bad date as the worst thing that ever happened. If you have the date from hell, you can turn it into a funny yarn for your friends. Maybe not tomorrow, but at some point. Don't take anything seriously, whether it's not finding anyone attractive to you or a string of dates that seem to go awry.
15. Constantly affirm that you are okay no matter what. You are okay even if dating makes you think of your ex. You are okay even if dating makes you think that something is wrong with you. No matter what happens, remember it doesn't matter and you are okay.

No matter how long you've been dating, keep these fifteen rules in mind. They will help you stay grounded and stay out of someone else's head. Keep your focus on yourself and on what is going on in the present.

The First Dates and Relationships After a Major Breakup

After a major breakup and then a period alone, it's tough to get out there again. There are a few typical reactions after your first few post-breakup dates:

1. *I don't like this person.* That's okay. Journal about why you don't like the person. Is it because this person is so different from your ex, or is there something about the person that is really not for you? Don't rush to judgment; make sure to give new people a chance. If this person truly is not for you, remember to set boundaries with him or her, and make sure that you end it politely.

2. *This person doesn't like me.* Again, reject the rejector. Do not take it personally. If you are taking rejection personally and feeling sensitive that someone doesn't like you, this may be a signal you're not ready to date yet. It's okay to date a few times and then come to the conclusion that you're not ready. If this is the case, get back to the work, but give yourself credit for putting yourself out there.

3. *I'm back in the throes of grief.* This can either be residual grief because dating signals that you really are moving on and turning the page, *or* it can mean you're not ready to date again. It depends. You might need to go on a second date or even a third before you figure out which one it is. Again, be gentle with yourself. If you need to pull back, do that. But don't think you'll never be ready. You just need a little more time.

4. *I'm going to be alone forever.* Dating can be hard and scary even when you are determined to make it light and breezy. In the face of this, it's easy to become negative. Dating brings us face-to-face with our worst faults and habits, and where we thought we were solid all of a sudden we can see nothing but what is wrong. Try to step back and recultivate a light and breezy attitude. When your attitude turns negative, it's time to take a break and do your affirmations.

5. *What in the world is still going on?* Use dating as a gauge to see what you still need to work on in yourself. Do you suddenly become someone else on your dates? Is your self-confidence still fragile? Are you trying too hard to make a date work? Are you pandering to the other person to make him or her like you? Journal about these issues, and consider them, but be sure you're doing it for you and not for someone else.

It's normal for dating to bring up some residual grief that you didn't know was there. I remember going out on a date with someone new and suddenly thinking of the guy I had broken up with six months earlier. We went roller-skating, and I went too fast and hit the floor. The guy was really nice, and took me to my car and said, "So, should we do this again?" I said, "What, fall on my face?" and he laughed and said, "No, go out." I said, "Okay." Then I got in my car and cried my heart out for my ex.

The ex was not someone I would have had a successful relationship with, yet I cried over him all night. I thought about calling him even though it had been months since we had talked. For several days I fought the urge to talk to my ex, and it took me a while to agree to go out with the roller-skating guy again. When we did go out again, I kept it light. Over the course of four or five dates, I realized I really liked him, and eventually thoughts of my ex faded away. I was with him for four years, and he was there for me and my kids in a way my ex never would have been.

But what happened later doesn't change the fact that after that first date, I felt terrible. Maybe going out with someone new signaled that I was moving on or it may have been residual grief. Whatever it was, it was meaningless because it had no bearing on how I felt about my ex or about this new guy. So, don't put any stock into after-first-date-with-a-new-person feelings for your ex—and, whatever you do, don't call your ex!

Don't put too much psychic energy into early dates. You don't know these people and they don't know you. You're still observing and you're still learning to learn. Go easy on yourself and give yourself credit for trying. You're ready to date when you can sit across from someone and think to yourself, "This is who I am. Now, let me assess *you* and figure out if I like you." This is a carefully cultivated mind-set that takes time to achieve, not a "put on" mind-set (where you don't believe it) or a haughty attitude (where your ego has run amok with it). Project self-confidence and believe it every second.

Relationships

If you've done your work, you are ready to think about a new partner and a serious relationship. When you wrote your inventories, you discovered a lot of information about your past and your relationships. Through that process you were able to see clearly what has been going wrong and what needs to go right. Hopefully, you have revisited your past and addressed the things that needed to be addressed. You have finished some unfinished business so that you're not dragging it into future relationships. You are a whole person with friends, interests, and good self-esteem. You've spent time alone and done some light dating. Now it's time to put what you've learned about yourself into action.

As with all your other goals, a relationship is something to work toward, not to jump into headfirst. Think about it, write about it, and plan for it. First, review your inventories and think about what you want in a relationship. Know what you stand for. Where are your lines? Where are your boundaries? What is acceptable or unacceptable? What is an absolute deal breaker? In what ways are you willing to compromise in a relationship? What are you not willing to compromise? Make new lists and think about what you want the future to hold for you.

The next step is to vow to be true to your beliefs, values, and standards no matter what. You want someone who will value you, and if you find yourself with someone who does not, then you need to be sure you'll let the relationship go. You may meet a lot of people you're genuinely attracted to, but who simply are not right for you. They may want to change you, or you may wish they were different in important ways. You may meet nice people who are lacking things that you find valuable. A nice person may take an interest in you, but after spending time together, you find there are too many incompatibilities. Let the person go. Don't try to fit a square peg into a round hole. Leave it be and move on. While compromise is essential to any successful relationship, compromising who you are in order to find love will completely block your success in life and love.

Healthy people know who they are and what they want, and they know the difference between giving up what's important and compromise. This may be a tough balance to strike at first, but with time you'll learn this difference for yourself. If you know yourself, you are more inclined and more able to come to the right decision for both you and your relationship.

It can be hard when you're in a relationship that doesn't feel quite right but that doesn't necessarily feel bad. In this situation, many people choose to stay until the relationship gets bad. But you don't have to do this. The relationship could be with a good person, but if it's not what you want, it's better to get out early than to cause a lot of pain later on. The relationship could be a dream, but if it's not your dream, it's fine to end it.

The Early Stages.

Within the first few weeks of dating someone new, you should be assessing your ability to be yourself in this relationship. Is this person taking up too much of your time? Do you have a standing evening out with your friends that you haven't been to since starting to date this person? One of my seminar students worked hard to get through her breakup, and eventually started seeing someone she thought was a nice, attractive man. After a few weeks, though, he showed himself to be jealous and overly involved in what she was doing. Although it hurt, she ended it and felt proud of her ability to take care of herself. Even though she feared she would never find anyone else, she knew that being alone was better than being with someone who is controlling and insecure. The work she had done paid off. Let this be you as well: Be aware of what's going on in your life, and believe in yourself enough to know when you're better off alone than with someone who is not a good fit.

In the beginning of a new relationship it's important to continue seeing your friends, working at your hobbies, going to the gym, and spending time alone. Yes, new love is wonderful, but you need time to assess it. Don't assume your friends will understand; don't think that you don't need to work out anymore or go to your painting class. Use time away from your new partner to examine your young relationship, both to determine if it's all you want it to be, and to determine if it's allowing *you* to be all you want to be. And if it's not, think again.

Is This Good Enough?

You get what you put up with, so remember your standards and your list of what is acceptable and not acceptable. Remember that "better than my last relationship" is not always good enough. My first post-divorce boyfriend wrote me a letter once after not speaking to me for weeks. I couldn't figure out why we weren't speaking—he had never bothered to tell me; he had just disappeared. I was thrilled that now here he was in paper and ink. Now he had written me a letter and all was right with the world! The letter said something like, "Don't give up. Take things one day at a time. Someday we'll be together. Absence makes the heart grow fonder." After weeks of moping and wondering what had happened to him, I ran to my therapist, who had tried to convince me to forget any guy who would just disappear like that. I marched triumphantly into her office and presented the letter as proof that he really did love me.

She read the letter, looked at my excited face, and tossed the paper on the table with a droll, "How original." The sound of my bubble bursting could be heard, I was sure, from several states away. I asked her angrily, "This is so much more than my ex would ever do. Why isn't this good enough?" She said if I wanted it to be "good enough" it could be, but if I wanted to be with a man who loved me, really loved me, this was not good enough, and "better than the last relationship" is not necessarily good enough. Only consistent, unconditional love is good enough. I had never heard of such a thing. I wasn't sure I believed it, but for the first time in my life I was beginning to understand the possibility that "good" might not be good enough. If I was willing to settle for less, then that is exactly what I would get. It takes a while to learn to be loved like nobody's business, but it starts with saying, "Yes, this is nice, but it's not nice enough. I want and deserve more." This is why you must stay true to your standards.

Keeping Your Standards High Even When You're Madly in Love.

I was once in love with someone who had been my friend before we ever became involved. We had a very close relationship, but we could not figure out how to see each other due to our very busy schedules. We had been in graduate school together and, during that time, had seen each other on school nights and every other weekend. Once we graduated, though, our schedules were completely incompatible. I suggested making a schedule, having set nights to see each other as we had had in school, and he hated the idea. I would propose something that I thought was rational, logical, and workable, and he would reject it out of hand and say we just needed to take it as it came.

After agonizing about the situation for a couple of months, I had to realize that this person simply wouldn't bend for our relationship, and I had to let it go. I also realized that no solution, except his, would work for him. He simply wanted it to be left day-to-day and would not agree to anything I said. Even though I slowly and methodically explained to him, repeatedly, that my life just didn't work that way, he wouldn't discuss it. I had three kids and three jobs, and had to plan my life. It just didn't work without a schedule. He gave no consideration to my concerns, being only content to fly by the seat of his pants and wanting me to do the same.

At one point during this time, I vented in frustration to a mutual friend of ours. He said, "Sounds like you're pushing glue up a hill." That described it exactly. It was hard, messy, and pointless. And it was time to stop.

Although breaking up with this man was one of the hardest things I've ever done, I could not go on feeling as if I was being strung along and unfairly accused of trying to "control" the relationship, being inflexible, and "making a big deal out of nothing" simply because I had proposed a schedule. I was tired of being insulted when I was trying to resolve our issue. No matter how good things had been with him, it wasn't good now. I couldn't take it anymore—it was wearing me down, wearing me out, and it was ridiculous.

I could only gauge how I felt and what he was accusing me of doing. I felt as if I wasn't trying to control him, as I was accused of doing, but trying to have some semblance of control over my own life. It's easy to get into defense mode when you are trying to take care of yourself and there is no book to consult on the particular issue you are facing. There is no book that says, "If your boyfriend does not want to work with you to schedule time together, then break up with him." I had to figure out, based on how crazy I was feeling, if this was acceptable to me.

It wasn't clear at the time, but after thinking long and hard and being satisfied that I had really tried to work it out, I let it go. This is the benefit of knowing yourself. If I had let him tell me that it was okay to go day by day, if I had convinced myself that he was right and I was wrong and controlling, I would have been miserable. Know your limits before you get into a relationship; it makes it that much easier to recognize when they've been passed.

After that relationship I went through a string of dating and "minirelationship" situations where I was unhappy with each person I was involved with. This one was cheap, and that one was cranky, and the other one was a flake. Friends of mine told me that I was too picky and that my standards were too high. But I'd decided I would rather be alone than put up with much of anything. Don't let others define you or tell you what "good enough" should be. If you let them, people will tell you all the time what is and is not okay, or what you're being "picky" about, or what you have no right to object to. Don't put your standards to a vote. Know what you like and what you don't like, and then stick to it.

Eventually I began to think that I would be alone, and that was okay with me. I have a picture of me and my boys from this period. My two youngest were graduating from eighth grade, and in the photo I am grinning and we are all hugging each other. I know I was happy in that picture. I was fine alone. I didn't know whether I would ever find someone who could meet my standards, and that didn't matter; it just mattered that I held true to those standards, no matter what.

Accept It, Change It, or Leave

During your time of grieving and your time alone, it is important to continually affirm that you deserve to be treated with love and caring. It is important to affirm to yourself that you will not accept anything less. To take care of yourself, you must learn to make choices. Whenever you are in a situation or confronted with an issue that is causing you pain, heartache, anger, or upset, you have three choices: accept it, change it, or leave. Think through all three. The one that is the *right* answer will reveal itself to you.

Accept it. Look at the situation, and realize there is really nothing you can do about it. You have tried to change it, and it doesn't change. People may tell you that you should leave but you're not ready to. Therefore, you have to work on truly coming to terms with the fact that this is the way it is and the way it is going to be. To accept something you must let go of all hope of changing it.

Change it. You can try to change the situation. If it's a relationship, you can go to counseling. If it's a job, you can transfer. If it's a home, you can move. If it's a family member, you can draw boundaries and set limits. Most people spend the most time in "change" and try, time and again, to change it, believing that it really will change. You need to be honest with yourself and consider whether you really can change it. Are you just fooling yourself into thinking you can change it because you don't want to accept it or leave?

Have you delivered an ultimatum? Never deliver an ultimatum you have no intent of following through with. Have you made it clear that if things don't change you are leaving? Or are you making empty threats? Are you talking until you're blue in the face? If you've already tried to change it and it's not changing, you have to decide between accepting it and leaving. There is no fourth choice.

Leave. If you've tried to accept it and cannot, and you've tried to change it and it's not changing, it's time to leave. It might be hard.

After you try, you might find it impossible, so you will need to go back to trying to accept it. Dealing with difficult situations is, well, difficult, but when you understand that there are only three responses, it makes it much easier. Don't spend too much time and energy on "change" if it's not really possible. Be honest with yourself and examine your motives.

Being with people and in situations that are easy to accept is the goal, so keep moving toward that goal. When you find yourself in less-than-optimum situations, decide what works best for you. The only other choice is to stay in a holding pattern by deciding not to choose. It means you spend your days (and nights) in confusion and indecision. That is not a permanent state, so don't treat it like it is. If you continually state, "I should leave but I'm not strong enough," that is deciding not to decide. At some point, at some time, you need to decide, and there are only *three* choices. Make one.

What Real Love Is and Is Not

> Love is an action.
>
> M. SCOTT PECK
>
> Real love is a permanently self-enlarging experience.
>
> M. SCOTT PECK

After you've done your inventories, you should be ready to put dysfunctional relationships aside. But perhaps you're unsure about what real love looks like. In short, love is as love does.

When I've asked my clients, my seminar students, and my blog readers what is the single most helpful thing I've said to them, "Love is an action" is in the top three on most lists. It astonished me when I first heard it—that what matters is what you do, not what you say—and I continue to see people who are amazed when they hear it and then use it as a parameter in life to evaluate whether people are loving or not. It's what you do, not what you say. The other thing that is important, they say, is the distinction that good relationships make your life larger instead of smaller. Dysfunctional, destructive love affairs make your life smaller because you lose important things such as sleep, family, friends, material objects, money, and time at work. You also lose self-respect, self-esteem, and your ability to think clearly and independently. But that is not what love is or love does. Dysfunctional relationships are not about love; they are about trying to win over the struggles of the past.

When you finally meet someone who loves you and respects you in words and actions, relationships take on a whole new meaning. Your life becomes bigger because the things you discovered about yourself in your alone time are still being honored and cared for and you have a partner to share your life with. Love accommodates you and all your interests and obligations. You're not being asked to give anything up for love and someone is helping to support you while you support him or her.

Real love, functional love, doesn't cause you to lose people, places, things, health, sleep, or appetite. Real love does not demand, either actively or passively, that you give up your friends, hobbies, or interests. In fact, it encourages independence and being fulfilled by other people, places, and things. When you are a healthy and functional person, your healthy and functional mate trusts and supports you. Your partner does not purposefully or unwittingly engulf you.

If you're losing your friends, your family, or your children due to a relationship you're in, you need to think about what is going on in this relationship. Don't automatically blame your friends, family, and children. If your partner always wants you to choose him or her over others in your life, even if it's not an explicit demand but always turns out that way, there is something wrong. Real love does not strip you of the things you love or the people you love, and real love does not make you choose. Real love encourages quality time alone with friends, family, and children. Being nurtured and loved by others makes a person fulfilled and, in turn, adds to the primary relationship.

Real love doesn't make you worry, wait, and wonder what will happen. In dysfunctional and destructive relationships, you are always waiting for the other shoe to drop. When you are unhealthy, that uneasiness captures your attention. As long as your attention is captured, you are not thinking about leaving or making your life better. Instead, you are always focused on your dysfunctional mate. It is hard to find the energy to leave while you are constantly embroiled in arguing or dysfunction.

Real love does not play mind games, does not send mixed messages, and is not passive-aggressive. If you're in a relationship where these issues are present, chances are you have felt a little bit crazy once or twice. Experiencing these things in a relationship eventually makes you feel so crazy you can't live your life to the best of your ability. This is damaging and narrowing, where love should be self-enlarging. If you find yourself in these situations, it is time to assess and get out.

In the 1970s there was a schmaltzy movie called *Love Story* that was advertised with the tagline "Love means never having to say you're sorry." Although it was to be a punch line for years, there is some truth in the much-maligned phrase. Real love doesn't need to apologize very often. This is not the same thing as saying that love *doesn't* apologize, because most controlling, angry people never apologize. Instead, real love doesn't *need* to apologize very often. Love is about taking care of yourself and taking care of your mate. And in real love, those aspects are in balance, so they seldom collide and apologies are rarely necessary.

Real love does not play games. It does not say one thing and mean another. It doesn't speak out of both sides of its mouth or set you up for failure or make it so you can never win. Real love does not constantly criticize and find shortcomings. Real love does not make you feel bad about yourself. Remember these things, and set your standards in the sky. Remember that real love continuously and consistently makes your life better. Settle for nothing less.

Putting It All Together

Whether you are learning to be alone, starting to date, or venturing into a new relationship, remember to stay true to yourself and all the work that you've done. Continue your work no matter what and you'll continue to reap all the benefits of it whether in or out of a relationship.

9

Letters from Readers and Frequently Asked Questions

These are some of the most common e-mails I receive from readers of the GPYP blog (http://gettingpastyourpast.wordpress.com) and students of the GPYP/GPYB seminars. Some of these are published on the blog and others are not. If you would like to send an e-mail to be answered on the blog, write to me at susan@gettingpastyourpast.com.

Letter Number 1: When They Blame You for "The End" and You Want to Take It All Back

I'm finding it almost impossible to face the reality of my situation and move past my past! I was engaged to a man but found several things that bothered me about him, though these things did not change the fact that I loved him. I had some doubts and delayed the wedding date. Eventually he said he didn't think it would work out and he went back to his ex-girlfriend!

I feel as if I pushed him away with my doubts and indecision. So I blame myself and can't get over it. But what kind of a man says he loves me and there is no other woman for him in the world and not even one day later goes back to his ex? I'd appreciate any kind of perspective you could offer me on this. I am still blaming myself and hoping he will come back to me. He still wants to be friends. Thanks

Realizing that things are going too fast and asking for a step back is a good and healthy decision. Better to stop and evaluate the situation than be tethered to the wrong person for years. It was not your decision, which was good and right, that brought things to an end. It's okay to have doubts and indecision, and a healthy couple will air them and talk them through. Obviously some part of you recognized that he is not "the one." Listen to that part of you that was barking. Empower it. Let it be heard. Do not try to crush it with blame for his departure. He departed because, as I like to say on the blog, he's a *bananahead*—not because you did anything wrong.

Instead of saying, "Let's see if we can fix what's not right" or "Let's talk about how to make us ready to set a wedding date" or even "Let's take a break for a while and think about things," he broke it off completely and went back to his ex. This is an unhealthy response, and if it's vindictive (which it might be), that is even worse.

Stop beating yourself up for making a wise decision. This guy sounds like a self-centered, spoiled loser. Do not remain friends with him. He seems to be a selfish person who is not capable of being your friend, only of doing what he wants when he wants.

You ask: What kind of a man says he loves me and there is no other woman for him in the world and not even one day after the breakup goes back to his ex? The answer is not a nice one, not a healthy one, and not one that you should want. Your loss is your gain. Thank heavens you didn't marry this guy. Forget him and work on yourself. You will do better next time.

Letter Number 2: MySpace Drama and Facebook Follies

I receive an e-mail every few weeks from someone caught up in a social-networking drama. No matter how many times I tell people to stay off their ex's social-networking page, they continue to "peek" and often are devastated by the results. The people who write are men, women, old, young. It's amazing to me that MySpace drama knows no bounds of age or gender or sexual orientation. I receive e-mail from folks of every possible group and background on a fairly regular basis.

Let me be clear that this is not a rant against MySpace. MySpace doesn't hurt people. People who use MySpace to hurt people hurt people. Social-networking tools are great if used as tools and not as weapons. But when they're used as weapons, people get hurt and those people need to learn to stay away from the thing that is hurting them: their ex's use of social-networking tools.

Have you been hurt by someone's ranking of you? Have you been demoted recently? Was your picture taken down? Is there a new person in your place? Are your insides churning? Are you tracking every movement your ex makes? Are you interpreting everything he or she does and trying to figure out which things are really secret messages to you? Are you putting things up on your page to make your ex jealous or angry or sad?

Well, stop it. Stop it. Stop it. Stop it.

Immediately delete your accounts at MySpace, Facebook, LiveJournal, Match.com, and other places where you and your ex tend to virtually "meet," or simply block your ex's page. You can recreate them all when you're all better, but you're not going to get better if you keep going there. If you don't want a haircut, don't hang around the barber shop!

Playing games through these or any other mediums is unhealthy. Healthy people don't spend their lives trying to send subliminal messages to people who may or may not be reading. Healthy people don't spend time trying to outmaneuver someone else by random ranking of vacuous people met in cyberspace. Healthy people don't sit around trying to figure out what a drop in rank *really* means. Healthy people say good riddance to bad rubbish and call it a day. So say good riddance and call it a day.

What are you looking at, anyway? What sort of information are you getting? How do you know that whatever is going on (your photo down, another's photo up, ranking, demotion, etc.) is even real? It's a false picture in the same way that vacation pictures are false.

Did you take pictures of breaking down on the side of a road in the pouring rain in a country where no one speaks your language? No.

You took pictures of laughing, smiling faces on a boat on a sunny day. What goes on your MySpace or Facebook page? *Look at us having a good time!* It's a skewed and often misleading picture. People don't put their fights, disagreements, and "the day I threw the iced tea at him and stomped out" on Facebook. They don't put their doubts, their pressure, their issues with their partner on MySpace or Facebook, and they don't invite people over to look at the slides of their recent falling-out. They show you the sunny side of the street, no matter who they are. Don't compare your insides to other people's outsides.

And how do you know you are not being manipulated to keep you in the game?

The only way to win is not to play the game. By participating in MySpace drama or Facebook follies, you are playing the game. We are not Pavlov's dogs on social-networking sites. Don't drool when the bell goes off (ranking or availability being the bell). If you are, something is wrong. You are programming yourself to look, wonder, whine, and stay weak when you need to be getting strong. The endless peeking and worrying is just going to deplete you. Remember the rules about going NC, stopping obsession, and staying out of someone's head? Peeking at a person's social-networking pages is staying in his or her head.

Step away from the keyboard. Go out for a walk (there's a whole world out there that does not exist in cyberspace!), write in your journal, call a friend. Do something constructive. Go back to the suggestions in Chapter 4. It is time to build a life of your own, not to compulsively check up on your ex. You must walk away and decide that you have had enough. Get a life and get off networking sites. Does it hurt when you do that? Don't do that!

Letter Number 3: Journaling and Writer's Block

This letter came out of one of my first seminars, which led me to incorporate the answer into future seminars as well as journal-writing workshops and audio lessons.

> *I really enjoyed your seminar and vowed to start journaling the next day, but I find myself unable to write a lot of the time. Is there anything I can do to get "unblocked"?*

This is something that happens to beginning and even experienced journal writers. Though you may feel you have a lot to write about, you still can't get started. When that happens, try one of the following techniques to get "unstuck."

1. Set a timer for ten minutes. Put a pen to paper and start writing. Even if it's nonsense or "I'm not sure what I'm writing," do it. Just keep writing without taking your pen off the paper, for the full ten minutes. The pen must be moving at all times. This is called stream-of-consciousness writing. It may seem silly at first, but if you insist on writing for ten minutes, things will eventually start to flow. Whether you're new to journaling or you do it faithfully every day, stream-of-consciousness writing is a good exercise now and again. It will uncover things you're not aware of and move you closer to healing.

2. Think about the best day you've ever had and write about what that day meant to you.

3. Similarly, think about the worst day you've ever had and write about what was going on, for you, on that day.

4. Pick a random date from years ago. Research the song that was most popular and what was making news that day, and try to imagine what you were doing then. Try to reconstruct where you were and where you had been. A coaching client of mine, who felt his thoughts and feelings about his past were "jumbled," recently started buying old magazines from when he was younger to kick-start some of his memories (both good and bad). He said, "Sometimes just looking at a single ad can trigger a host of memories and feelings I could not seem to get in touch with on my own." Look at old commercials or television shows that you liked growing up. Just write about these innocuous things and see where it takes you.

5. Develop the habit of jotting down different things during the day to jump-start your journaling process at night or the next morning. If you're at work, e-mail yourself at home, or leave a message on your cell phone, or carry a notepad or small memo pad and write things down as they come to you. Develop a routine to record your observations during the day.

6. Make your journal and your journaling process your own. One of my students keeps very detailed records of what she does each day as well as places she's been, who she's talked to, even meals she's had. She enjoys her journal as her own project. Another man shared that he likes to draw in his journal and said:

> *I am able to express myself better by doodling or sketching in my journal. I once went to a café and began writing in my journal. To end my post for the day, I tore out the restaurant logo on the paper serviette and pasted it on my journal. I bring my journal anywhere I go. So my journal tends to have little "souvenirs" I took or bought from the places I went pasted on it.*

These are great ideas that can help you make your journal work for you in the way that you need it to work. Make it your own!

Letter Number 4: When You Are NC and Your Ex Contacts You

Recently I received the following letter:

> *Three months ago I took your advice and went NC. It was hard at first but the sporadic correspondence with my ex had been making me crazy. So I put him out of my thoughts, journaled a lot when I was tempted to break NC, and joined some groups to meet new people. Everything was going well. Then late one night, he sent me a text message asking if I wanted to talk by phone or on the computer. I was stunned but didn't respond. The next day I was a nervous wreck and my mind was suddenly back where it was three months ago. Once again, he's on my mind all the time. I'm wondering what he wanted. I'm thinking of things I want to say to him. I'm not journaling or going out. I'm just staying home trying to figure out what to do about contacting him. I'm not even sure I want to but I don't want the opportunity to pass me by. Maybe he was just bored or couldn't sleep, but part of me wonders if he really wanted to know how I was doing or maybe he wanted to see me. I feel as if I'm back to square one with NC. It's so hard all over again. Help!*

This letter is so common that I have a pile of similar e-mails from readers who become unhinged when the ex makes contact after a period of no contact. Some feel angry or intruded upon; for others, it brings up painful feelings about the breakup. Still, some welcome engagement, wanting to tell the ex off or just to hear what he or she has to say. Still others would like to be reassured that they are missed or discuss whether there is a possibility for a friendship or even a reconciliation. No matter what the reaction, the letters have a universal refrain: This person's contact has upset me and I'm thinking of breaking NC.

Before you do that, take a moment to regroup. Unexpectedly hearing from an ex after time has passed can be upsetting. Before you do anything about it, allow yourself time to get over the surprise of the contact and then give yourself time to cycle through the many different emotions and thoughts you probably have. Then it's time to regain perspective by remembering the following:

1. It doesn't matter that your ex broke NC. You are the one who is resolved to stay NC. He or she broke NC. You may be understandably upset, but you don't need to act on it. Just spin, go through the various emotions, and let it be okay. But don't make contact!

2. There is no reason to be the victim of other people's whims. Take charge of your own life and stop acting like some random phone call or e-mail threatens everything you've worked so hard for. You don't want to ever give someone else that much power. Not now; not ever again. Don't be a victim. Learn to take control of your own life. Choose your own destiny and don't allow others to choose it for you.

3. Unspoken communication is not a reason to make contact. You may want the opportunity to convey all the things you've thought of since the last time you spoke to your ex, but you know the drill. If you feel you have something to say, journal it, talk to a friend, or go to therapy or a support-group meeting.

4. Review the positive and healthy reasons you've chosen NC. You are not NC in angry silence *at* your ex. You are not NC to show you are strong or to prove any point. You are NC for your own growth and healing. NC is about *your* dignity, *your* space, and building *your* new life so you can live well and find someone who does love you and care about you.

After the contact, it might take a couple of days to get back to where you were, but you will get there. You might feel every emotion for a few days, but you don't have to act on it at all. Remember, if your ex breaks contact, do not respond. I repeat, do not respond, at all.

Letter Number 5: Anniversary Grief

A longtime reader and seminar student wrote:

> *I have been doing really well, but the first anniversary of our breakup is approaching. I'm not sure what to expect. Can you talk a little bit about anniversary grief?*

Everyone is different. Some people pass the anniversary of the breakup as if nothing happened. For others, it can provoke a huge recycling where you can find yourself, suddenly and inexplicably, in the emotional soup. The most violent "re-dunking" typically occurs at the first anniversary, but you can have anniversary reactions at other intervals.

Anniversary grief is normal. It's the marking of the severing of a significant relationship. It's the remnants of what remains behind. It's more sloughing off of memories—the connectedness, as well as the pain of disconnecting. It's a marker in your life of something and someone that was once important.

Human beings are creatures of habit. We all tend to live by calendars, and our lives are marked by dates and occasions. We celebrate the people in our lives and we gather in groups during certain times. Part of how we survive as a species is by forming connections and a sense of community with others in large and small groups. Community dates like New Year's (world community), Fourth of July (American national community), winter holiday (personal/religious community), birthdays (family community), and anniversaries (couple community) mark the ebb and flow of our lives. Sometimes we celebrate with the world, other times just with one other person, and every group size in between. But we mark dates, celebrate them, and get into rhythms and patterns around them. It's how we are. We are somewhat hardwired to have dates matter as markers of our lives.

So an anniversary of a loss is another marker. We grieve not only for what was but for the "date" that we have to recognize and then extinguish. It's why people feel a draw to connect with an ex on a birthday (both their own and their ex's) even if, logically, it makes no sense.

Before you get to integration and acceptance, you must first experience the whole gamut of letting go. And part of that experience is observing the empty place markers, understanding that something significant has come and gone, and feeling the feelings that go along with that. It's tempting to try to stop the recycling. You've already spent an enormous amount of energy on this person, this loss, this experience. You've been feeling better, and life is starting to feel like life again. You don't *want* to feel the anger, the sadness, and the loneliness. No one wants to go back there, but if you fight it, it only gets worse. So allow it to happen and know it doesn't last forever.

After the first anniversary recycle, things get so much better. Just honor your process, allow the last remaining remnants of grief to flow out, and in no time you will be back to the life you've worked so hard for in the last year. A few weeks later the person who wrote the letter above wrote to say she was feeling much better now that the anniversary had passed.

Know that anniversary grief and recycling is a necessary, but short-lived, bump in the road, and you will come out on the other side stronger and happier. And while you're experiencing anniversary grief, remember to be good to yourself—today and always.

Letters Number 6 through 12: Success Stories

In the short time since I started the GPYP blog, I've been privileged to witness remarkable transformations from people who use the tools and work the program. This is just a small sample of the letters I've received and some of the comments on my blog.

> While the breakup experience will always be in the back of my mind, it just does not hurt anymore. A time came quietly and subtly when all the hard work came together. Since my last breakup six months ago, I've done a lot of soul searching and grief work. My dating history consisted, entirely, of short-term, doomed relationships that I mourned constantly. With the help

of the inventories I (finally) realized that all of my pain, and even most of my relationships, were the result of unresolved grief. There were so many broken (non-romantic) relationships in my life that I never fully grieved, and so every breakup with every loser I ever dated felt like the end of the world, even though they were only ever the end of doomed flings with broken/defective men.

Where am I now? Well, completely over the last relationship (have been for a long time, actually). But even more importantly, I've worked through a lot of underlying issues that landed me in my last failed relationship. In the past few months I've been on several dates with different men that haven't gone anywhere. And whenever I find myself getting overly upset about someone not calling, I remind myself that it's not this situation I am upset about, it's more than likely something from the past being triggered. I journal and move on.

The really good news is that I've rejected some bad ones that I might have embraced in the past. All in all, I look at where I am now and compare it to where I was last year and I am a totally different person. I feel stronger and wiser and a lot more stable. When I do panic (for instance: "I'm never going to meet anyone . . . I'm going to end up alone.") I tell myself that it's just panic and not based in reality. I feel like I am in a good position to meet someone good and to actually know that I've met a good person when it does happen. And so doing the work may not be easy, but it's definitely worth it.

■ ■ ■

I felt something was wrong with me for having needs that went beyond fun and drinking. I felt like I was a wet blanket or a morose person because I wanted to talk to him about future plans or commitment. Well guess what? After two years together, it's perfectly normal to want to know if the relationship is going somewhere.

My point is, I never thought I would get over him. Sometimes I feel a snag of disappointment when I think of him. But it got to a point where I had to choose to be with someone who wouldn't meet me halfway. The choice was about choosing to settle, or choosing myself. You should always be the first choice. Always. When you get there, you're "over" the relationship. Get to a point where you're not apologizing for your wants, your needs, your "issues." Get to a point where you know your issues and you've sat with them and sifted through them and integrated them. As you do this, your ex will begin to fade into the back of your mind. As you become your own priority, s/he will not be able to occupy as much space in your heart or your head. You don't need someone to validate your existence —because guess what. You are here. You exist. It's not really a question of proving that you deserve to be. You already are.

■ ■ ■

It has been a long time since I posted. I used to leave messages several months ago. I had a bad breakup nearly a year ago. My girlfriend left me as all other areas of my life were collapsing. Fast-forward to now. I am not currently seeing anyone, and I really haven't been on many dates. I started my MBA and I've maintained a 4.0 GPA.

There are two very important things that I have learned:

1. No contact. The sooner you adapt to this and adhere to it, the sooner you'll start feeling better.

2. You cannot force love. Since my breakup, several people I know have met someone when they were least expecting it. I met my ex after forcing, and forcing, and forcing trying to meet someone, which in the end didn't work out anyway. This time around, I am just going to let it happen on its own.

■ ■ ■

Lots of tears were shed about loss, people, dreams, hopes, goals, disappointments, and nothing at times. The nothing tears became a welcoming cleansing to me. It was like pushing off the weight of the world. I took up walking at first, then running. I journaled all the time, like an obsession. I paced the floors, I stared at the walls, I talked to friends, I slept when I was tired, I woke when I wasn't, I purged everything that reminded me of my ex, and did much more recommended here by the wonderful souls on GPYP.

What kept me going and made it easy for me to practice NC was I really trusted the process. I was curious to find out what it was like to get through that dark tunnel and see for myself what everyone was talking about.

There are no really big moments . . . it's quiet, and eventually, you love hanging out with yourself more than anyone else. You must arrive at grief's door to pass through it. It's a wonderful gift to share how we all got from there to here.

■ ■ ■

My one-year "freedom from the ex" anniversary is approaching next month, and it's unbelievable how much different my life is now. The disastrous relationship and worse ending literally changed my life and gave me a new perspective on everything. So as much pain as it all caused me, I am beyond grateful for it.

It took me a while to finally meet someone who fits well in my life. Prior to finding your blog and attending your seminar, I was just looking for someone who would "put up" with me. After doing my work and seeing my patterns, I realized I was such a doormat! No wonder women walked out on me. After doing the inventories, I was happily single and then started looking for someone who wanted a decent guy and didn't want to play games. Instead of rushing to my next relationship, I took my time and chose carefully. Now I'm moving toward a committed relationship with a healthy woman. Things are good!

■ ■ ■

I really believed you when you said I had a "broken chooser" and the only way to fix it was to do the inventories and start observing those I was attracted to. It was not easy by any stretch of the imagination. But I started to change and grow and noticed the people I was attracting were so much healthier than those who came before. After dating a while, using your "Healthy Dating" guidelines, I am now seeing one man exclusively and things seem to be pretty good. My usual way is to give up my whole life for a man, but not this time. Not only does he understand my need to have other activities, but he encourages them! I will never again make someone else my entire world. Thank you for all your help!

My last letter is from a woman who was one of the first readers of the blog who absorbed the GPYP principles like a sponge. We talked often via e-mail and I met her at one of the seminars. She is a beautiful woman who now has a healthy marriage with a loving man. Her letter touched me and I wish the same success for all of you:

Dear Susan,

As you know, I stumbled upon your GPYP blog and e-mail support group during a breakup. At the time, I may have seemed like a successful, "together" woman to many people in my life. But inside, I was hurting deeply and my relationships were unfulfilling. I had overdeveloped defense mechanisms and underdeveloped boundaries. I believed self-care was selfish and affirmations were either arrogant or a wishy-washy waste of time. I was often anxious, sad, or angry. I was stuck in relationships that recreated the triangulation in my family of origin. I had old grief and no idea how to finish it. I know you have followed my grief recovery, but I write you this personal note today to express my enormous gratitude for all you have done for me and so many others like me.

In the last decade, I made some headway in individual and group therapy. But with your advice, example, and encouragement, I have done no less than transform my life. I have read and/or interacted on your blog almost daily for well over a year. I have participated in your e-mail group. I used what you taught me to look my past in the eye, grieve what was not so great and what never was, and find gratitude for the good parts. The result is that I know myself better, I love myself more,and I feel genuinely empowered.

As an extension of all this self-improvement, I am building a stronger, more authentic relationship with my sister and enjoy a healthy, satisfying relationship with a wonderful man. I will continue to learn, but the dramatic paradigm shift has happened, and I feel that I am forever on course for a lovely life. I know I am strong and able to work through the inevitable challenges of the future.

They say that when you are ready to learn, the teacher will appear. . . . Susan, you are the real deal. Thank you for being my teacher and my friend.

With love,

Kathy F.

AFTERWORD

Keep the Good Things Working in Your Life

Remember that the key to moving on is balance—working the bad out while working the good in. Learning to be good to yourself while processing your grief is not easy, but it's always worth it.

Please join us on the GPYP blog and sign up for seminar notices. Interacting with a supportive community is so important to building your new life. Please know you are welcome to join us online and in person!

I hope this book guides you to a new and healthy life. Stay true to the following eight things and you will land in that life very soon:

1. Always keep the focus on you.
2. You get what you put up with.
3. Does it hurt when you do that? Don't do that.
4. Reject the rejector.

5. Remember: It doesn't matter, it doesn't matter, it doesn't matter.

6. Be good to yourself.

7. Love is an action.

8. You can do this!

BIBLIOGRAPHY

Ackerman, Nathan. *The Psychodynamics of Family Life*. New York: Basic Books, 1958.

Adler, Alfred. *Understanding Human Nature*. Center City, Minnesota: Hazelden, 1998.

Ahles, Scott R. Our Inner World: A Guide to Psychodynamics and Psychotherapy. *Baltimore: Johns Hopkins University Press, 2004.*

American Psychiatric Association. *Diagnostic and Statistical Manual of Mental Disorders*, 4th edition. Washington, DC, 2000.

Ansbacher, Heinz and Rowena. *Individual Psychology of Alfred Adler*. New York: Basic Books, 1964.

Beattie, Melody. *Codependent No More*. New York: Ballantine Books, 1987.

Beattie, Melody. *Beyond Codependency*. Center City, Minnesota: Hazelden, 1987.

Beck, Aaron. *Love Is Never Enough: How Couples Can Overcome Misunderstandings, Resolve Conflicts, and Solve Relationship Problems*. New York: Harper and Row, 1988.

Bowen, Murray. *Family Therapy in Clinical Practice*. New York: Jason Aronson, 1978.

Bowlby, John. *Attachment and Loss Vol. 1: Attachment*. New York: Basic Books, 1968.

Bowlby, John. *Attachment and Loss Vol. 2: Separation: Anxiety and Anger*. London: Penguin, 1973.

Bowlby, John. *Attachment and Loss Vol. 3: Loss: Sadness and Depression*. New York: Basic Books, 1980.

Bradshaw, John. *Bradshaw On: The Family*. Deerfield Beach, Florida: Health Communications, 1996.

Corsini, Raymond J. and Danny Wedding (Eds.). *Current Psychotherapies*. Itasca, Illinois: Peacock, 2005.

Craighead, Linda W., W. Edward Craighead, Alan E. Kazdin, and Michael J. Mahoney. *Cognitive and Behavioral Interventions: An Empirical Approach to Mental Health Problems*. Boston: Allyn and Bacon, 1993.

Dinkmeyer, Don and Gary D. McKay. *The Parent's Handbook: Systematic Training for Effective Parenting*. Bowling Green, Kentucky: Step Publishers, 1997.

Ellis, Albert. *Feeling Better, Getting Better, Staying Better: Profound Self-Help Therapy for Your Emotions*. Atascadero, California: Impact, 2001.

Freud, Sigmund. *The Standard Edition of the Complete Psychological Works of Sigmund Freud*, ed. James Stachey. London: Hogarth, 1957.

Goldenberg, Irene and Herbert. *Family Therapy: An Overview*. California: Brooks/Cole, 1996.

Edelman, Hope. *Motherless Daughters*. New York: Addison-Wesley, 1994.

Estes, Clarissa Pinkola. *Women Who Run with the Wolves*. New York: Ballantine, 1992.

Festinger, Leon. *A Theory of Cognitive Dissonance*. Palo Alto, California: Stanford University Press, 1957.

Greenberg, Jay R. and Stephen A. Mitchell. *Object Relations in Psychoanalytic Theory*. Cambridge, Massachusetts: Harvard University Press, 1983.

Haley, Jay. *Strategies of Psychotherapy*. New York: Grune and Stratton, 1963.

Haley, Jay and Lynn Hoffman. *Techniques of Family Therapy*. New York: Basic Books, 1967.

Horney, Karen. *Our Inner Conflicts*. New York: W.W. Norton, 1945.

Hughes, Judith M. *Reshaping the Psychoanalytic Domain*. Berkeley: University of California Press, 1990.

James, John and Russell Friedman. *The Grief Recovery Handbook.* New York: HarperCollins, 1998.

Kubler-Ross, Elisabeth. *Death: The Final Stage of Growth.* New York: Simon and Schuster, 1975.

Leick, Nini and Marianne Davidsen-Nielsen. *Healing Pain: Attachment, Loss and Grief Therapy.* New York: Routledge, 1992.

Lendrum, Susan and Gabrielle Syme. *Gift of Tears: A Practical Approach to Loss and Bereavement Counseling.* London: Tavistock, 1992.

Lerner, Harriet Goldhor. *Dance of Intimacy.* New York: Harper and Row, 1990.

Lewis, C.S. *A Grief Observed.* New York: Bantam Books, 1963.

Lindemann, Erich. "Symptomatology and Management of Acute Grief." *Journal of American Psychiatry.* Vol. 151 no. 6 (1944).

Minuchin, Salvador and H. Charles Fishman. *Family Therapy Techniques.* Cambridge, Massachusetts: Harvard University Press, 1981.

Neeld, Elizabeth Harper. *Seven Choices: Finding Daylight After Loss Shatters Your World.* New York: Time Warner, 2003.

Norwood, Robin. *Women Who Love Too Much.* New York: Pocket Books, 1985.

Norwood, Robin. *Letters from Women Who Love Too Much.* New York: Pocket Books, 1991.

Parkes, Colin Murray. *Bereavement: Studies of Grief in Adult Life.* London: Tavistock, 1972.

Peck, M. Scott. *The Road Less Traveled.* New York: Touchstone, 1998.

Rando, Therese A. *Grieving: How to Go on Living When Someone You Love Dies.* Lexington, Massachusetts: DC Heath, 1988.

Rando, Therese A. *Treatment of Complicated Mourning.* Champaign, Illinois: Research Press, 1993.

Raphael, Beverley. *The Anatomy of Bereavement.* New York: Basic Books, 1983.

Scaturo, D. J. et al. "The Concept of Codependency and Its Context within Family Systems Theory." *Family Therapy* 27 (2): 63–70, 2000.

Sills, Judith. *A Fine Romance.* New York: Random House, 1978.

Tice, Louis E. *A Better World, a Better You: The Proven Lou Tice "Investment in Excellence" Program*. Upper Saddle River, New Jersey: Prentice Hall, 1989.

Wanderer, Zev. *Letting Go*. New York: Random House, 1987.

Winnicott, D.W. *The Child, The Family and The Outside World*. Boston: Addison-Wesley, 1987.

Yalom, Irvin D. *The Theory and Practice of Group Psychotherapy*. New York: Basic Books, 1985.

INDEX